Mother's Intuition?
Choosing Secondary Schools

by

Miriam David, Anne West and Jane Ribbens

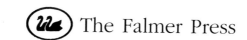 The Falmer Press

(A member of the Taylor & Francis Group)
London • Washington, DC

UK The Falmer Press, 4 John Street, London WC1N 2ET
USA The Falmer Press, Taylor & Francis Inc., 1900 Frost Road, Suite 101, Bristol, PA 19007

First published in 1994

A catalogue record for this book is available from the British Library

Library of Congress Cataloging-in-Publication Data are available on request

ISBN 0 7507 0286 9 (cased)
ISBN 0 7507 0287 7 (paper)

Jacket design by Caroline Archer

Typeset in 10/12pt Garamond by
Graphicraft Typesetters Ltd., Hong Kong

Printed in Great Britain by Burgess Science Press, Basingstoke on paper which has a specified pH value on final paper manufacture of not less than 7.5 and is therefore 'acid free'.

Mother's Intuition?
Choosing Secondary Schools

Contents

List of Tables

Foreword

A generation ago, social scientists who worked in the field of education, were, in the main, concerned with such matters as social class and educational opportunity. In those seemingly distant days, the operation of the 11 Plus Examination and the differential rates of 'staying on at school', provided a rich field of enquiry for social scientists, most especially as that field carried with it important implications for the development of social policy in the field of education. Overall, the issues appeared relatively clear. The crucial points of selection within the educational system, operated in general terms in favour of middle-class children, and though there were subtler forms of interpretation that were from time to time investigated, for example, number of siblings, region, child's date of birth and length of schooling were shown to be significant factors in educational performance, the overall message relating to social class was consistent. The 11 Plus Examination, rates of staying on in secondary education, entry into higher education, all favoured children from middle-class homes, and though there was some attempt to look at gender differences, these were not regarded at that time as of great significance in policy terms, and matters of ethnicity seemed not to matter at all apart from some American studies.

It was essentially on the basis of the social class and educational opportunities studies that many of the educational changes of the 1960s were implemented. Many of those changes were designed specifically in the hope of remedying the social class inequalities that had been identified within the educational system. It is not the place here to dwell on those organizational and administrative changes, but what can be said was that by the late 1960s and early 1970s, the social scientific study of education had broadened significantly, away from matters relating to structure and access, towards the curriculum and the internal organization of schools. Partly, at least, that move was occasioned by the apparent success of the earlier social class studies in changing policy. Over time, however, it became clear that those liberal reforms of the 1960s and early 1970s, produced far less radical change than had originally been thought. The inexorable forces of social class still dominated educational performance, and many of the supposed benefits and reforms affected relatively few individuals. Moreover, other issues relating to gender and ethnicity had, as a result of social changes, forced themselves upon the attention of social scientists and policy makers.

By the early 1980s many of the reforms in education were discredited as they had failed to realize the aspiration of the 1960s. Throughout the 1980s and into the 1990s in this country, a radical Conservative Government has attempted to introduce the benefits of market forces into a range of Public Sector activities, and education was to be no exception. Clearly associated with the benefits of market forces, is the concept of parental choice. In classical economics, the operation of the market was made possible by freedom of information and freedom of movement. It seemed obvious to the Government therefore, that one of the ways forward in education was to introduce an element of market competition and to make much more information available to the public and, specifically, to parents about the organization and performance of schools. It seemed sensible also to 'free' schools from the domination of centralized local authorities, and make as many of them as independent as possible of local bureaucracies. Thus, throughout the 1980s and early 1990s, a variety of measures have been taken, which have seemingly given to parents, much more information about schools, about the curriculum, about examination performance and the financial standing of the schools. At the same time, governors in the schools have been given much more practical and financial independence to manage the affairs of the school in conjunction with the headteacher and staff. The key element in all of this, however, is the concept of parental choice. Parents, it is assumed, know what is best for their children. Parents need to be well-informed in order to make choices and will behave in the best interests of their children, most especially in seeking out schools which will be characterized by good order, successful teaching resulting in good examination results, and with good records of pupils moving successfully into higher education, further training or employment. Good schools will be approved of by parents and flourish, others will not, and will have to improve or perish.

What the authors of this study have done, is to try to examine how that process of parental choice might work in practice, if not on the ground, at least in the various living rooms of a range of homes. Miriam David, Anne West and Jane Ribbens, have paid particular attention to the role of mothers in making secondary school choices, and have identified as well as social class, gender and ethnicity as important variables in the way that choices are exercised.

The conclusions of the study, based both on qualitative and quantitative data, indicate that parents and mothers most especially, take their responsibilities for choosing schools seriously, and that in many cases, the child is also involved in some way. The concerns that the parents express, are indeed those that the Government and policy makers may well find sensible, even attractive. Parents want for their children, when choosing a school, the kinds of things which those who inspired the most recent legislative changes seem to expect them to want. The problem, however, is that families differ in their ability to find the processes by which they might achieve those worthwhile objectives. The message that emerges from the study, indicates that the differences that families face when dealing with a variety of economic and social markets, is maintained in this modified form of the educational market. The better off the family, the better educated the family, the more likely they are to be able to successfully realize their choices for their children. The study itself is a model of clarity and represents a good example of collaboration between two major educational institutions, the London School of Economics and South Bank University. Moreover, the study fits well into the range of work that has been developed at South Bank University by Professor Miriam David and her team. The study exemplifies the changing concern in social science and in the analysis of social policy which has resulted in those fields being drawn back to their concerns of the 1940s and 1950s. The harder-nosed times of the 1980s and 1990s have given rise to increasing concern about access, opportunity and outcomes than was the case in the sixties and seventies. This study represents an important contribution to the analysis of those issues and is a further significant addition to that body of work relating family values and life to social policy for which South Bank University is becoming noted.

Professor Gerald Bernbaum,
Vice-Chancellor,
South Bank University.

Acknowledgments

We have worked collaboratively on this project, pooling ideas and sharing the various aspects of the work of designing the study and interview schedule, the execution of the analysis and writing of it into a book. Miriam David and Jane Ribbens have worked in this way on a previous publication, together with two other colleagues and were therefore happy to propose it. We recommend this type of collaboration to others, and, indeed, hope to repeat it with our new research project funded by the ESRC, also on parental choice and involvement in education.

We would like first of all to thank the Leverhulme Trust for giving us the grant which enabled us to carry out this study, and we would also like to thank the Centre for Educational Research at the London School of Economics, the former Department of Social Sciences and now the Social Sciences Research Centre at South Bank University for housing the joint project. We would also like to acknowledge our gratitude to the Directors of Education in Camden and Wandsworth and their staff for enabling us to carry out our interviews in their primary schools. The headteachers and teachers of the six schools are also gratefully thanked for facilitating our work and allowing us access to both the parents and pupils whom we studied. Above all, we would like to thank the parents and pupils without whom this study could not have taken place.

We could not have carried out this piece of research without the invaluable help and assistance of Jean Hailes for interviewing and data analysis and Audrey Hind, who was extremely helpful in the earlier stages of analysis of the study.

Finally we would each like to thank our families, especially our children — the seven boys and girls on whom we based our intuition — both for their inspiration for this work and for their forbearance with us for being so pre-occupied, as mothers so often are, with our concerns for their upbringing and well-being.

We would like to dedicate this book to all of our children in the hope that they will take forward our aims and seek to accomplish a more moral and just world.

Introduction

Contexts and Concepts: Parental Choice or Chosen Parents?

Aims and Objectives

'Mother's in charge of choice of school' was the *Evening Standard* headline reporting on the official results of our Leverhulme research project (11 May 1993). Indeed, our aim had been to explore who in the family context made the choice of secondary school and also to look at how that choice was made and/or negotiated amongst various family members. We were particularly interested in whether gender made a difference amongst parents and/or children about choice of school and the different factors that were taken into account by families when thinking about the process of changing school from primary to secondary. We were also interested in whether a range of social factors such as social class, ethnicity and/or race, or formal religious affiliation or belief affected these processes and decisions, if such they were. In *Choosing a Secondary School: The Parents' and Pupils' Stories,*' we reported on our survey of primary school parents and pupils in two London boroughs in the immediate post-ILEA era and we produced our initial report for our funders, the Leverhulme Trust (West, David, Hailes, Ribbens and Hind, 1993).

This book builds upon the quantitative analysis presented in the published report and provides a more in-depth study of the parents and pupils. It is about the ways in which families go about the process of choosing schools and, specifically, how parents make choices about the secondary schools to which to send their children at the end of state primary schooling. We also look at how the children are involved in the process of choosing. We do not look at the results of the process in terms of what happens when children go to their secondary schools but we were rather more interested in the factors leading up to the 'choice'.

We wanted to problematize the concept of 'choice' which has become a key notion in current politics especially around consumerism. It is a theme which seems to be becoming increasingly important throughout Western societies, as Bjornberg observes.

> To a growing extent, women and men are adopting a cultural model
> of individual choice . . . The individual is to choose his/her own options
> in creating his/her welfare. (1992, p. 6)

As a concept, 'choice' is integrally linked to the theme of 'the individual' and
the ideology of 'individualism' (Bellah *et al.*, 1985).

> The self is not merely enabled to choose but obliged to construct a life
> in terms of choices, its power and its values. Individuals are expected
> to construct the course of their life as the outcome of such choices,
> and to account for their lives in terms of the reasons for those choices.
> (Rose, 1989, p. 227)

Yet the concept of 'choice' glosses over a number of difficult underlying
dimensions, such that its blessings may in reality be quite mixed (Baker, 1994).
    We explore the choices made from a quantitative perspective and we
address the issues in a more qualitative vein, trying to shed light on the complex
processes and reasonings for the choices ultimately made. We are concerned
to show that making a choice, especially such a momentous one of a child's
school, is not a simple decision but involves a complex set of issues and may
involve a variety of family members. Moreover, the question of what constitutes
a 'family' and therefore who is involved is no simple matter. Instead the notion
of family covers a diversity of social relationships. We are able to present some
of the basic quantitative factors but we also try to tease out the complexity of
the processes by illustrating the ways in which we tried to listen to family
members and analyse their feelings in a more qualitative fashion. We are
particularly concerned to go beyond some of the common-sense notions about
these processes, such as that reported in the *Independent* on 18 November
1993 when discussing the new league tables of all schools that 'choice' may
be based on 'mother's intuition', although this may indeed be relevant.
    This study then relies on a mixture of methods to illustrate our argument
that choice is, in itself, a very complex topic and not one that is easily susceptible
to analysis or simple presentation of the issues. Moreover, it is further complicated by the fact that families themselves are complex phenomena and may
be infinitely varied and not subject to simple quantitative analysis.

Outline of the Chapters

In this introductory chapter we outline the various contexts in which our study
was set and we discuss the various approaches to studying the notion of
parental choice. In Chapter 1 we discuss the ways in which we selected our
methods for studying parental choice and then move on to discuss our selection
of schools, parents and pupils. In Chapter 2 we discuss the characteristics of
our sample of parents of 'target children' in terms of social class, ethnic and

family backgrounds and circumstances. We also raise their earlier education and upbringing. In Chapter 3 we debate the question of who in the family took responsibility for the 'decision' about school choice and discuss the relationships between parents and children over this matter. In Chapter 4 we move on to look at the ways in which parents were informed of the procedures for transfer to secondary school from the last year of primary school and we analyse their own approaches to looking at the processes and procedures.

In Chapter 5 we broaden our discussion to look at the reasons parents offered for their choice of particular secondary schools, using evidence from previous research studies about the various possible factors that parents might bring into consideration, such as academic performance, results or reputation versus a child's happiness and the location of the school. In Chapter 6 we discuss both the other side of the coin — factors that would militate against parents selecting particular schools — and broader concerns, such as their approaches to the issues of order and discipline. We present a lengthy discussion of discipline because this was one issue of salience to all parents, although the way it was considered varied amongst parents.

In Chapter 7 we widen our discussion even more to consider the ways in which the parents used their own prior experiences of schooling and education to inform their consideration. We also address their current 'political' and educational concerns and their hopes and expectations for their children's futures. In Chapter 8, we consider the pupils' own perspectives and stories about their views of, and involvement in, the processes of 'choice'. Finally, in Chapter 9, the conclusion, we draw together the many threads and try to reach some conclusions about the ways in which we now understand the processes of school choice and the responsibilities for selection or decision-making amongst and within families.

The Various Contexts for the Research Study

The study is set in a number of important contexts; it is based on two local education authorities (LEAs) in post-ILEA (Inner London Education Authority) London and took place at a time of major change in national educational policies towards more 'parental choice' of education in the early 1990s. We undertook the study to explore whether or not the current policy debates about parental choice in education, markets and consumerism were at all salient to particular groups of parents and families in primary schools in inner London at the time. We were also interested in the broader context of the debates about policy changes.

On the one hand, policy issues about parental choice of school were located in wider debates, raised by the Conservative government, about the transformation of social and educational policies from public and state provision and bureaucracy towards consumer choice in a market situation. Indeed, the ideological underpinnings of policy by the New Right administrations in the

1980s and early 1990s focused specifically on creating markets in public and social services and transforming users into 'consumers' or 'customers'. These debates were not confined to the British context but have their parallels and similarities in other western industrial or, rather, so-called postmodern societies. It is particularly the case that in the USA, Canada, Australia and New Zealand questions of political and social citizenship and consumer choice are being raised in the political arena. In some, if not all the countries cited, it has been New Right administrations that have sparked the debates, especially with respect to education (Guthrie and Pierce, 1991; Ginsburg, 1992; Kenway *et al.*, 1993). However, the ways in which changes in public policy delivery are being transformed from public to private, voluntary, charitable or even family agencies is not confined to education but is a vital characteristic of social and political transformations in an international context in the late twentieth century.

On the other hand, these debates were being raised by right-wing politicians in Britain at a time of major social and economic change, including particularly changes in family and cultural diversity. These kinds of societal changes are also part of far wider social and economic processes on a transnational scale and tend in the direction of individualism rather than collectivism. They are often dubbed as part of postmodernism or critically appraised in this context (Giddens, 1992; Ribbens, 1994 forthcoming; Taylor-Gooby, 1994). They have also been raised as a serious matter for political change by both New Right politicians and social critics in many industrial societies (Berger and Berger, 1984; Halsey, 1992; Davies, 1993).

We hope, therefore, to contextualize our relatively small-scale and detailed study of parental choice of state schooling in these wider discussions about social fragmentation, individualism and consumerism in postmodern societies. We also aim to address their implications for social and educational policies and practices as well as the more theoretical relationships and linkages.

The Political and Social Scientific Research Context

In Britain, there has been a great deal of academic social scientific, as well as media, interest in the policy developments of the 1980s and early 1990s, particularly around educational reform. The media, for instance, have tended to focus on the questions about changing national policies in order to improve educational standards. They have also become involved in the processes of contributing to the wider political and policy debates by producing their own league tables of schools (and other educational institutions as well as other social or public policy institutions) to aid the processes of educational choice and decision-making. In fact, there has developed a complex interplay between media and government over how best to judge educational standards and achievements and contribute to the processes of decision-making in families. Moreover, the media have begun to play a part in deciding what constitutes educational standards, which are as much to do with judging the performance of educational institutions through their teaching staff as they are with judging the performance of pupils/students and attempting to raise their educational standards.

Nevertheless, the league tables in the press do not seem to have contributed significantly to changing practices in that they have mainly been produced in the quality rather than tabloid press and have focused on middle-class values and aspirations. To that extent, they have also tended to concentrate on high levels of public examination attainment in both the public and private sectors (particularly selective schools) and have not focused on the processes of secondary schooling. In other words, they have been concerned with specifying examination results for GCSE and A levels, on the assumption that parents are most concerned with academic results as a basis for choosing schools. This has been fuelled by the government who, in the 1992 Education Act, required the production of media presented 'league tables' of both examination results and truancy rates of schools from 1993 onwards.

Examination results are one of the main issues relating to how parents choose schools that we will explore below in Chapter 5. It is interesting, however, to note at this juncture that the debate about league tables has taken on a recent new twist, in that the government has conceded their inappropriateness at certain ages and stages (namely ages 7 and 14), given the reports of Sir Ron Dearing, the Chairman of the School Curriculum and Assessment Authority. He had been invited by the Education Secretary on 7 April 1993 to review the scope of the national curriculum and its assessment and testing system. In other words, the question of examination results and league tables remains a thorny issue of debate that has been susceptible to pressure from parents' groups and governors, as well as teacher unions and teachers themselves.

Much of the academic social scientific debate about changing educational policies especially around choice and markets has, in Britain, focused upon the context of the changing legislation, first in Scotland and later in England, as noted elsewhere (Macbeth *et al.*, 1986; Adler *et al.*, 1989; Coldron and Boulton, 1991; Glatter and Woods, 1993; David, 1993). Curiously, compared with social scientific research in the previous period of social democracy, it is rather administratively dominated and not so concerned with social processes. But researchers have also raised issues about the concept and implementation of the notions of choice and the creation of markets and/or quasi-markets in education amongst other social policy issues (Bowe and Ball, 1993; Le Grand *et al.*, 1993; Ball, 1993). As a result of this kind of detailed analysis and approach there is now a good deal of evidence about aspects of the processes of change and choice over different levels and types of education in a number of areas and regions of Britain and the UK and in contrast to other industrial societies. As a prelude to conducting this research study, David embarked upon a wide-ranging review of the literature and debates about policy developments which summarizes a great deal of this evidence and to which we will have occasion to return (David, 1993).

There has, however, been very little concern about the impact of these changes on families and those in different or changing socio-economic or cultural circumstances (David, 1993). Indeed, most of the research has only raised the issue of the impact of changes on the parents through LEAs and schools, whether LEA maintained or financed directly from central government or through a partnership between business, and whether primary or secondary schools. Much of it focuses on the management of the change process from the point of view of either educators or education managers and administrators. It is highly specialized and largely linked to managerial or bureaucratic questions of a specific kind (Edwards *et al.*, 1989; Glatter and Woods, 1993).

We set out to try to reverse this kind of approach and look at what parents thought about choice and the processes to which they were subjected when their children were in the final year of state primary school. Given the burgeoning educational research, it is curious that little of it has emphasized these questions or 'problematized' notions of parents, consumers or choice. However, that may have to do with the fact that the traditional focus of educational research has been on educational effectiveness and the emphasis is therefore on the role and workings of the educational institution rather than the perspectives of family members (Mortimore *et al.*, 1988; David, 1993; David *et al.*, 1993). Indeed, this is a common feature of research around family issues; it is the policy agenda and resulting perspective that predominates, while the agendas of family members themselves go unrecognized.

We were also particularly interested in the concept of the *family* and the ways in which family and cultural diversity might influence the processes that went on at home as well as at school — the various interactions between mothers and fathers and their children. We also knew that in London, especially the inner London boroughs, there is evidence of a great variety of family patterns and cultures, particularly as mediated by religion and ethnicity and/or race. This kind of evidence has emerged from surveys commissioned in the days of the ILEA (Hargreaves, 1984; Thomas, 1985). It has also been the subject of much academic analysis and scrutiny (Brannen and Moss, 1991; Joshi, 1991; Solomos, 1993).

Moreover, we knew that while there has been considerable continuity in certain aspects of family life there have also been trends away from traditional nuclear families towards different family households, reconstituted families and towards an increase in lone parent families, particularly lone/single mother families and ones in which there are considerable amounts of maternal employment (Brannen and Moss, 1991; Wicks, 1991; David, 1993). We were eager to explore whether these had any effects on the processes and patterns of choice and decision-making in families over schools. We were particularly concerned with whether or not the policy changes were having any impact on the lives of parents, especially mothers, in difficult and straitened circumstances. We were surprised that, despite the massive numbers of particular research studies on parental choice, none had thought to 'problematize' the concept of *parent* in terms of gender, race/ethnicity or family context. It remained the case that all the studies addressed the question of family and parents through social class and/or ethnicity only by means of socio-economic indicators such as parental or family background or circumstances (David, 1993; Ball, 1993).

At a more theoretical level, we were also interested in the extent to which changes in family structures/contexts, such as lone parenthood or reconstituted families, and characteristics, such as race and/or ethnicity, affected the traditional notions of social class influences on education. We wanted to explore the meanings of education and schooling for a particular group of parents at what has traditionally been considered a time of decision-making. Was it in fact the case that parents — either mothers or fathers — give a great deal of consideration to different factors over the choice of a secondary school for their child? Or was it more a matter of the parents — mothers and/or fathers — seeing the processes of education and schooling as contributing, relatively automatically, to the types of school to which a child moves from the primary to secondary school stage?

The ERA and the Current Research

The current research was carried out after the passing of the 1988 Educational Reform Act (ERA), well before the 'major' changes towards more markets and consumerism in education. The ERA 1988 built upon the 1981 Education Act in respect of parental choice. The latter had allowed for *parental preference* of school but in the context of the LEA's efficient use of resources which also included the setting of 'planned admission levels' to LEA schools to balance size within the locality. It also allowed for the publication of school prospectuses and information about schools to assist with the expression of parental preferences. This itself had built upon the 1944 Education Act and its subsequent amending legislation to ensure that parental wishes were met and children educated according to their ages, aptitudes and abilities, but in the context of efficient use of public resources. John Patten, the Secretary of State for Education, and author of the White Paper entitled *Choice and Diversity: A New Framework for Schools*, described the prehistory of educational policy prior to the 1980s as one of 'deadening uniformity' (1992 Cm 2021). In other words, he contrasts public bureaucracies with internal markets in education, or what Le Grand has recently called quasi-markets (Le Grand *et al.*, 1993).

Thus the ERA of 1988, in his view and that of the government, widened the notion of parental choice by creating a range of different types of school. In addition to private or independent schools and the local authority system of schooling of state-maintained or voluntary-aided or controlled schools, it allowed for schools to 'opt out' of local education authority (LEA) control and become 'grant-maintained' schools (GMSs) and it also allowed for city technology colleges (CTCs) to be established. Moreover, it changed the nature or character of those schools remaining within the local authority ambit. It abolished the notion of planned admission levels (which targets numbers at lower than full physical capacity) and replaced it with the idea of 'open enrolment' whereby schools are required to accept a higher number of applicants, with the number limited only by physical space. However, research by Morris (1993) points out that there is a great diversity of assessments of school capacity and LEA officers are 'greatly concerned at the continuation of three or four quite separate methods of calculating it'.

It also required LEAs and schools to publish more extensive information through booklets etc., as a basis on which schools could be chosen. State schools themselves became more autonomous from the LEA through financial and managerial changes and delegation of funding of schools through local management of schools (LMS). Most important with respect to parental choice, however, was the idea that parents, through a parental ballot of the parental body, could be involved in the decision about whether a school should remain in LEA control or become grant-maintained and funded by central rather than local government.

These various and varied changes were quite complex and the process of creating grant-maintained schools was rather bureaucratic. Research by Halpin *et al.* (1991) and Fitz (1991) has revealed how slow the changes have been. But the balance of power between parents and schools — at least in theory, as far as choice of school is concerned — has altered considerably in the direction of parents as the significant, if not main, decision-makers. In any event, these changes in organization have been accompanied by massive changes in the curriculum and the assessment of pupils through the national curriculum and assessment within state primary and secondary schools, also prescribed in the 1988 ERA. The focus of the 1988 Education Reform Act was not only on organizational change but also on changes in pedagogy; a combined process that has been characterized as 'market forces versus central control' Whitty (1990) (Lawton *et al.*, 1987; Ranson, 1990). We chose, however, to start our study of changes in educational organization in this period of massive educational as well as other organizational changes.

It is only subsequently that organizational changes and the more extensive creation of consumerism and markets in education have become the paramount issues in educational reform (Lawton *et al.*, 1987; Ranson, 1990). These massive changes in educational policy, away from local government support for schools towards a variety of different types of school funding, or what have been called quasi-markets, have now been seen as the central feature of educational reform (Le Grand, 1991). Thus our study was designed before Major replaced Thatcher as Prime Minister and started upon his policy of consumerism through the Citizen's Charter in 1991 (Page and Baldock, 1993). It therefore predated the Parent's Charter for Education, entitled *You and Your Child's Education* (1991) and the spate of subsequent legislation that was attendant on this, namely the 1992 Education (Schools) Act, the White Paper *Choice and Diversity: A New Framework for Schools* (Cm 2021, 1992) and its subsequent legislation, namely the 1993 Education (Schools) Act. Taken together, all these subsequent developments create a new system of markets and customers in education and all other social policies (Ranson, 1993; David, 1993b; Tritter, 1994).

Nevertheless, given our methods and approach we hope to be able to shed light on the key issues for families in changing circumstances about choices of education.

Conceptual Issues about the Study of Parental Choice of Secondary School

Before designing our study we decided to look further at two sets of questions about the concept of 'choice': first, can parents indeed be regarded as consumers in relation to their children's education and second, what is choice and diversity? The notion of parents making choices — to assert their wishes with regards to their children's education — requires some careful analysis to consider its meaning and relevance. For example, as Bell and Macbeth (1989) point out, in theory, whenever children attend school at all, parents have 'chosen' to send them since they do have the right to educate them 'otherwise'. However, it is hard to defend this usage of 'choice' when parents themselves may be unaware of, or unable to activate, any such alternative. Is it also stretching the notion of 'choice' too far to apply it to situations where a child is sent to the third or fourth school listed by the parents (Macbeth 1984)? Thus the University of Glasgow study (1985) preferred to use the term 'placement' as the overarching term, potentially covering processes that could be variously described as choice, allocation and selection.

What is it that parents are choosing between? Is there any real sense of choice and if so, what is its nature? Choices could cover a whole variety of educational matters, from choosing between schools attended, to issues within the school itself such as the subjects taught, the teaching methods used, or the individuals who do the teaching (Nault and Uchitelle, 1982; Macbeth *et al.*, 1984; Raywid, 1985). Here we shall concentrate only on choice between different secondary schools.

The concept of choice is also intimately linked to that of diversity, as the government acknowledged with the title of the White Paper as a prelude to the 1993 Education Act. But there are various other conceptual arguments to be made about diversity and national integration/cohesiveness (*cf.* Hirschman, 1981; Crittenden, 1988). How far are parents choosing between spam, spam and spam? Echols *et al.* (1990) found that in Scotland:

> Choice among state schools also increased with the options for choice, other things being equal . . . The options for choice explained a larger fraction of the variation in choice among state schools than of the variation in choice of the private sector. (p. 215)

If parents do not want spam, can they gain financial support for something other than spam? Bell and Macbeth (1989) distinguish between 'weak' and 'strong' choices, pointing out that the UK has in the past tended to provide weak choices, where someone else decides the options available. This may be contrasted with, for example, Denmark and the Netherlands, where parents can set up their own schools and get government funding for them (Macbeth *et al.*, 1984; Bell and Macbeth, 1989). Thus, parents can create their own alternative forms of schooling if they so wish. This is now becoming an option that the government wishes to encourage (Bowe and Ball, 1992; Whitty *et al.*, 1993). Macbeth *et al.* (1986) distinguish broad variations in the policies within the European Community towards school choice from:

- full choice (where schools have to adjust to accommodate everyone who wants to attend, for example Belgium, although parents cannot later change their minds once the school year has started), through
- filling the gaps (where schools have to grant a place to those who apply if there are spaces available within the school, for example England and Wales), to
- choice at the discretion of the local authority, without any national rules laid down (for example Denmark).

Crittenden (1988), however, points out that the existence of alternative schools may not just reflect a straightforward response to parental demands for diversity, being strongly affected also by pressure led by local community leaders, for example, of particular religious or ethnic groups: 'The existence of an ethnic group's schools may depend more on the effort of its leaders to preserve the group's identity and vitality than on the wishes of parents' (1988, p. 6). Options may also be strongly affected by other practical issues, not just legislation and policy decisions. Thus geography may be highly significant, either by effectively ruling out any alternatives to the nearest school (University of Glasgow, 1985), or by providing a vast array of alternatives, as where parents in New York City can choose between 'some 360 different magnet programmes in more than 90 different buildings' (Jackson and Cooper, 1989, p. 268).

Economic factors may also be highly significant in limiting choices, not only in relation to paying school fees but also in relation to transport costs, for both state and private sectors of schooling (Darling-Hammond *et al.*, 1985; Stillman and Maychell, 1986). For the majority of parents, proximity is crucial, particularly at the primary stage (see West, 1994 for a review of recent research), alongside a number of other issues — for example, the perceived academic record of the school, the perceived discipline in the school, the child wanting to go there (West and Varlaam, 1991) and local contacts via children's siblings or friends (see for example, Coldron and Boulton, 1991). Consequently, they cannot be regarded as necessarily choosing between a great variety of options. Rather, for many parents, there is a tendency to stay with a local school, unless this tendency is overridden by very strong reasons for rejecting the school (discussed further below). The other side of this particular coin though, is the anger expressed if parental choice asserted by other out-of-area parents prevents attendance at the local school (Strickland, 1991).

Another question to be addressed is whether or not the schools are also engaged in a consumer-oriented production process. How far can schools themselves be seen as responding to consumers? If parents are to be truly acting as consumers, then administrators have to be truly acting as producers: 'to make their schools special, to recruit openly and forcefully for parent interest, and to organize their schools in various ways to reflect local markets' (Jackson and Cooper, 1989, p. 269). But are schools both able and willing to respond in this way to the exercise of parental choices? The conflict here is between *exit* (i.e. consumer/economic behaviour) and *voice* (i.e. collective/political behaviour), in communicating to schools what it is parents actually want to change about schools (Hirschman, 1981). Thus producers may not know how to respond to 'exit' because this is a very imprecise form of communication. Consumers may never have been offered what they really want in the first place, and exit alone will not express this. A number of unconnected 'exits' from different schools may cancel each other out overall, allowing parents to exercise choice but failing to ever 'voice' to the schools the reasons for the various departures. Stillman and Maychell (1986) found that 'in numerous LEAs no information about why parents preferred some schools over others reached either the education officers or any of the schools themselves' (p. 183). Whether this is still the case, however, is by no means certain given the current pressure to increase pupil numbers and hence funding.

Do parental choices actually have an effect at a collective level? There are conflicting views here; Bell and Macbeth (1989) suggest that parental choice has a very minor effect on school rolls ('for all but a small minority of schools' p. 16), whereas Tweedie (1989) expresses considerable concern at the effects on school rolls. Are schools able to change to suit parental choices? Headteachers do not appear to think that they *should* change in this way in response to parental preferences (University of Glasgow, 1985). In other words, is the obverse of parental choice 'chosen parents', that is parents who are in some way 'chosen' by the schools and/or teachers? This is a point that Whitty *et al.* (1993) make strongly in relation to the creation of city technology colleges in a chapter entitled 'Choosers or Chosen?'

It is possible for 'choices' to be seen both as *threatening* professional autonomy by allowing parents to question professional judgments about a child's education, but also as potentially *enhancing* professional empowerment at the expense of administrators, as in the Minneapolis Southeast alternatives project which combined choice with decentralization (Raywid, 1985). Other systems may seek various ways of combining parental choice with professional expertise, as in Germany where children receive professional assessments before they transfer to secondary school, so that parents can be better informed in the choices they then make (Macbeth *et al.*, 1986). However, this issue of the relationship between parental choice and professional authority is not always very well thought through, as Crittenden (1988) comments in relation to Australian educational policies.

Yet another question to consider is whether parents are realistically described as active and assertive decision-making 'choosers'. 'Choice' is a term that denotes active decision-making (University of Glasgow, 1985), but how far do parents regard themselves as having real scope for decision-making, and how far do they feel able to be assertively active consumers? In what senses do they 'actively choose'? If the procedure requires them to list schools in order of priority, how do they actually view this procedure — how many schools do they actually put down, do they actively prioritize all of them or only the first one listed? If they know that a school tends to be oversubscribed, do they still actively consider it at all? If they put down the closest school, does this mean that they have not really considered any alternatives? How far does this idea of active choice necessarily reflect parental interest, that is, might parents *not* exercise active choice but still have considerable interest in the child's schooling? In other words, how do we assess the existence and signifi-cance of 'non-choice'?

Placing requests do seem to relate to social class and parents' education, although there are also a high number of placing requests from the skilled working-class groups (Nault and Uchitelle, 1982; Echols *et al.*, 1990). Even within the strictly defined sense of choice laid down within the current Scottish educational system, 3.5 per cent of the parents interviewed by Echols *et al.* (1990) were not sure whether or not they *had* exercised choice over their child's secondary school. On the other hand, Stillman and Maychell (1986) found that 'the act of filling in a form stating a preference, regardless of whether the choice is between similar or different schools, is sufficient to give the feeling of having been offered a choice' (p. 154). Yet 'the percentage of parents who felt that they had been given a choice ranged from 26 to 84 per cent' (p. 187). Simply having a choice does seem to lead to a more active search for information about schools (Nault and Uchitelle, 1982).

Nevertheless, Hughes *et al.* (1990) found that 45 per cent of primary school parents interviewed found the whole idea of being a 'consumer of education' to be a puzzling one, and half the parents did not see themselves in this way at all. Amongst those 34 per cent who saw themselves 'to some extent' as consumers of education, there were various reservations expressed in using the term. These included the feeling that assertions of parental power undermined the sense of trust between parent and teacher, and the view that parents themselves are producers within the educational system: 'not entirely like buying a packet of biscuits, you're putting in as much as you're taking out' (parent quoted by Hughes *et al.*, 1990, p. 14). There may thus be a desire to work with and in response to teachers, rather than make demands of them, but also potentially a sense of vulnerability in relation to teachers: 'at present, if I moan and groan it will be a rod for [my child's] back' (parent quoted by Hughes *et al.*, 1990, p. 17).

Certainly parents do not seem to regard themselves as powerful in relation to schools, not least because they may feel they have limited knowledge of what is actually happening to their children in daily school life (Ribbens, 1990;

Spey, 1991). Evidence from studies of client rights in other contexts also suggest that people may not use their rights to protect their own interests, either through lack of administrative skills, or through a fear of antagonizing officials (reviewed by Tweedie, 1989). There is a degree of variation in the actual procedures by which parents could express a choice, which related to whether LEAs had a policy of providing minimal or maximal choice to parents (Stillman and Maychell, 1986). How do parents and children understand the placement procedure? How far are they aware of the choice and appeals procedures, and of the criteria used to assign places in oversubscribed schools? To which parental characteristics does this awareness relate? Do parents believe they have any real choice *in practice*?

A more pragmatic set of questions also needs to be considered here. Does the system actually permit choice in practice? Even within all these constraints, does the system actually let parents assert their choices when they try to do so? If not, parents may perhaps be better described as expressing preferences rather than making choices (Stillman and Maychell, 1986). The same point has been made by Morris (1993) in his study for the Association of Metropolitan Authorities. Stillman and Maychell found that the vast majority (about 86 per cent) of parents who knew which school they wanted for their children had obtained a place at it a year later, although 'we still do not know how much the parents' choice had been conditioned by the LEA's arrangements' (1986, p. 187). More recently, press coverage suggests that the English system is disappointing parents more than the Scottish system, where 96.7 per cent of parents' school requests were granted in 1985 (Tweedie, 1989). There has been, at least in Britain, a degree of variation in the published criteria for allocation of places in different areas (Stillman and Maychell, 1986). The criteria actually used in practice to allocate places in oversubscribed schools seem to be obscure or at best, highly variable, once the published allocation criteria have failed to reduce the numbers of candidates sufficiently (University of Glasgow, 1985; Strickland, 1991). Even so, this could indeed be the intention of the system, if the aim is to really treat parental appeals individually (Stillman and Maychell, 1986). But there is a lack of official national statistics in England and Wales to reveal in detail how policies are operating in practice. It is, however, worth noting that the research cited above (Morris, 1993), which involved a survey of LEAs to which 69 responded, did not demonstrate that 'choice' was becoming more limited. However, successful first preference has been high and so scope for improvement has been limited: 'Some decline of numbers of successful first preferences has occurred, notably in urban areas' (p. 29). He also found the numbers of appeals to be increasing, but the proportions of successful appeals to be declining.

A further set of pragmatic questions relates to how far the whole issue has been localized and the variabilities within this and the extent to which this may be further extended. There is some evidence of the significance of localized historical situations (Stillman and Maychell, 1986; Echols *et al.*, 1990):

local authorities differed enormously both in their educational policies and their administration of school allocations and . . . the root of this variation seemed to lie in the existing variety of LEA procedures upon which the 1980 Act and 1981 Regulations were superimposed. (Stillman and Maychell, 1986, pp. 5–6)

Further, we need to consider the significance of local networks and communities in mediating parents' interactions with schools (Bell and Ribbens, 1994; Jackson and Cooper, 1989). This may occur in both directions, with such networks acting as powerful influences shaping parents' perceptions of schools (discussed further below), but also as significant channels which shape whether, and how, parental 'voice' is heard by the school (e.g. as seen in the William Tyndale dispute in Britain; David, 1978). Thus, Echols *et al.* (1990) note the significance in particular areas of a concentration of educated parents who want to exercise school choice.

There are also interesting questions about how people decide to live in particular areas, what are their images of these areas and how does this tie in with the parental populations of particular schools? Ribbens, for example, has experience of a particular primary school attracting a disproportionately high number of parents of certain political persuasions, which seemed to be partly to do with parents' perceptions of the type of community the school served. Nault and Uchitelle (1982) suggest that in the particular localities they studied in the USA, people had often moved into the area because of the type of community it was.

There are also considerations to be given to the different avenues of choice. Different income groups may exercise choice (where they seek to do so) in different forms such as through purchase of education in a particular system/ school (although note that private education may represent an *absence* of active choosing — Darling-Hammond *et al.*, 1985; Fox, 1985), through purchase of housing in a particular area, or through the exercise of rights through the legislative/administrative system. Bell and Macbeth (1989) point out that 'the legislation made the system marginally more egalitarian by opening up choice to those who were not home-owners' (p. 16). Darling-Hammond *et al.* (1985) also found that in the USA the most active choosers were parents who sent their children to state schools, with the choices exercised via their decisions about where to live, while low income parents sought to exercise choice through alternatives made available by the state. This study also found a significant relationship between the mother's educational level and use of the residential avenue for school choice. Thus, only 31 per cent of non-high school graduate mothers had taken choice of public schooling into account in their choice of residence, compared with 72 per cent of college graduate mothers. The linkage between residence and choice of school may also operate in more complex ways, according to the ways in which people, the type of local community and the school itself interact (as discussed above). Ironically, therefore, some of the recent British disputes about giving priority to local children may represent a conflict between people who have sought to exercise choice through alternative routes, that is either by moving house into the preferred area and then asserting the right of choice through proximity, or using the new legislation to challenge the priority based upon proximity.

Sallis (1988) discusses some of her own hesitations about assessing the value of choice: 'these bright but fragile baubles of choice and freedom whose edges are so sharp when they shatter' (p. 282). Hirschman (1981) suggests that economists have been over-inclined to favour exit rather than voice as a way of achieving efficiency, and furthermore, that exit may have particular costs to the consumer in some situations where exit may be very disruptive.

Given all the issues outlined above, parental choice may lead to advantages for some schools, and for the minority of children whose parents make active choices, by maintaining the rolls of such schools and boosting the attainments of some such pupils. Thus parental choice in Scotland has operated overall in the direction of older schools that had previously been selective, with a higher socio-economic intake (Echols *et al.*, 1990). Since there is a relationship between individual children's attainment levels and the overall socio-economic composition of the pupil population of a school (known as the compositional effect), Echols *et al.* conclude that 'Of itself, therefore, parental choice could tend to benefit the attainment of the pupils who move, but without that movement's raising average standards of attainment for all pupils' (p. 217). There may also be real disadvantages for others, by increasing social segregation between schools,[1] and inequalities between individual children: 'Our findings . . . confirm the fundamental sociological tenet that voluntary individual behaviour is socially structured in ways that reproduce inequalities between groups (Echols *et al.*, 1990, p. 218).

Parental choice can lead to increased social inequalities either by leaving some children with reduced educational opportunities in the schools that lose pupils, or else by allowing other pupils access to a superior education that is not open to all. Thus, diversity without open enrollment may lead to inequalities associated with restricted access, as with magnet schools in the USA (Raywid, 1985). Such differential processes also do not operate in a vacuum, but may exacerbate and increase already existing inequalities. It appears within varying areas consistently to be parents of the ablest pupils who are most likely to exercise choice, while marginal students may become isolated in 'alternatives that become dumping grounds for the weakest' (Raywid, 1985, p. 462). The different philosophical arguments for and against the values of parental/family authority as against state authority in the education of children are complex and may at times be finely balanced (Crittenden, 1988). The ways in which these issues are played out in practice may well vary in different countries according to the detailed form of parental choice legislation (Tweedie, 1989), which determines the precise balance that is struck between individual choice and collective needs. Thus, differences in legislation between England and Wales on the one hand, and Scotland on the other hand, have led to a marked difference in the extent to which the legislation has altered admissions policies in these countries: 'Scottish authorities grant parents' school requests even though the pattern of requests has undermined the authorities' ability to provide quality education in all their schools' (Tweedie, 1989, p. 182).

In a detailed study of the effects of this change in procedures in one area, Tweedie concluded:

> Their decision to refuse requests only when schools were filled to capacity thus excluded the Region's concerns for balancing enrollments, building links between schools and their communities, and ensuring that each school had pupils with a full range of academic abilities . . . This loss of pupils through parental choice occurred at schools that served the more disadvantaged areas of the city. It resulted in higher per pupil costs and restricted curricula at these schools. (Tweedie, 1989, p. 188)

The notion of parents as consumers may thus benefit a few and disadvantage some others. Overall, however, the notion may simply be irrelevant to the ways in which many parents view their role, and may thus leave untouched the issues that concern the majority about their children's education.

Broader Matters in Relation to the Notion of Parental Choice

We may also raise broader questions about how the processes of 'choice' occur — not just in relation to conceptual, political or administrative matters but in relation to choice over time. What are the processes for families by which placements or 'choices' actually occur? First, we need to consider timing and processes over a period. In relation to secondary school choices or placements, how far does this follow on from and depend upon earlier decisions made about education, either in relation to this child or other children in the family/household (for example, in terms of which primary school was attended)? At what point in time are school choices or placements considered by parents? Is it only at normal transfer age or at other times also? How early on do parents start consciously to consider secondary school placement or selection?

Second, we need to give consideration to *who* actually decides. How are decisions made within the family/household; what is the relative importance of the various household/family members such as the child, mother, father and siblings? Macbeth *et al.* (1986) suggest that the ultimate arguments for choice 'must remain those of parental responsibility for the child's education and liberty of conscience' (p. 36).

Yet the other side of responsibility is authority, and in this sense an alternative argument can be made, as to whether it is right to view children as extensions of parental authority. Does this incline towards a view of children as the possessions of their parents, and if so, where does this leave the rights of the children themselves as separate individuals (Baron *et al.*, 1981; discussed by Walford, 1991)? Stillman and Maychell (1986) found that just over half the parents did not discuss the choice with the child, even though children were said to have strong views on the topic, but the child's own wishes do tend to get cited as a significant issue by parents in a variety of studies, if not having the final say (Elliott, 1981; Coldron and Boulton, 1991; West and Varlaam, 1991). However, there may be class differences here, as West (1992a, 1992b) failed to find the child's own wishes coming up as an important factor in her work that examined private school choice, and Ball *et al.* (1994) found that for working-class parents the child's wishes are more often decisive, while for middle-class parents the child's input into the choice process is more limited.

Although in some studies children themselves appear to believe that their own views do count significantly (Walford, 1991), other studies have found that the children are active in the process of selecting a secondary school. West *et al.* (1991) for example, sought the views of pupils due to transfer to high school and found that two-thirds of them reported that both they and their parents chose the school, with nearly a fifth saying that they had made the choice and 16 per cent saying that their parents had made the choice. It seems likely, therefore, that there is a period of negotiation between child and parents in most families. If children are acting as the consumers rather than the parents, is this a good thing or a bad thing? Arguments can go both ways, but in either case, is this what legislators really had in mind? As Walford notes, 'there is little evidence for equating "popular" with "good" in terms of parental choices, and none at all in terms of the choices of ten year olds' (1991, p. 73).

There are also major considerations yet to be explicitly raised, concerning the nature of the 'choice' and 'decision-making' process itself. We have already noted Macbeth's (1984) preference for the term 'placement' instead of the word 'choice', as a more accurate and relevant description for the procedure by which particular children end up attending particular secondary schools. The political rhetoric of parents as 'consumers' implies freely acting agents, collecting and evaluating information to be able to make a clear decision in the best interests of the child in the light of the available evidence. There are a number of questions to ask here however. First, insofar as there are information gathering activities undertaken, what kinds of information do parents seek and through what routes; who else is consulted? What part do exam results play in the judgments parents make, for example? Second, and more fundamentally, how far is the decision-making process a rational, purposive and strategic activity at all, and how far a more impressionistic and slowly evolving process such as through discussion via 'the grapevine', or children's peer group ideas? There is now substantial research (to which our own findings contribute) to show that the placement decision occurs as part of a much wider network of social interactions, particularly between parents and children in general in the locality, interactions which are used both as a source of information and a source of more impressionistic judgments about the 'reputations' of schools. Third, what is the relevant time-scale in all this? If we concentrate on the information gathering processes, our own evidence suggests that this largely happens in the child's last two years at primary school. But if we consider some of the underlying orientations and values that parents hold towards the educational system, we will provide evidence of the deep feelings that surround parents' own memories of schooling, and their relevance for the type of educational experiences they want for their children. An overall theme of our study, then, has been to broaden the focus to be able to view the 'choice' process within a much wider context, as much a social process as a rational decision, potentially operating over a wide time-scale.

There is already considerable evidence for the significance of interactions between parents as part of decision-making as a social process. The grapevine was found to be important by Elliot (1981) in one study of one particular secondary school. The parents who already had sent children to the school were influential and it was more a grapevine than a single source of information, but the major factor was parents 'going to see for themselves'. Other parents at the school were the single most frequently cited source of information in Nault and Uchitelle's study (1982).

Stillman and Maychell (1986) found parents roughly evenly divided in their views as to whether or not primary school heads had been helpful in the process of choosing a school. Apart from the child her/himself, parents most frequently referred to other parents with children at secondary school, family, friends and neighbours, as other people they had talked to about the choice. Almost half had not visited any schools before making a choice, although just over half had seen at least one school brochure. These results differ somewhat from those obtained by West and Varlaam (1991) who found that just over a third of their sample of parents who were interviewed just before making their 'preference' had not read any brochures and the same proportion had not visited any secondary schools; these differences may well have been as a result of the changing climate in relation to the issue of school choice.

Stillman and Maychell also found that almost a third (60 per cent) had not seen any school examination results. If they had seen some exam results, a third (33 per cent) had seen them in school brochures or heard about them from teachers, 15 per cent in local newspapers, and 17 per cent from friends, people at work, and other parents. Where parents did make use of officially supplied information, 40 to 47 per cent found they only confirmed what they already felt, while only around a third found them most useful.

Finally we need to give consideration to the significant issues that parents cite in relation to decisions about school choice or 'placement', and what these relate to. There are few studies of children's own reasons for wanting to go to particular schools and not others. Walford's (1991) study of children in the first city technology college (Kingshurst CTC) cited fear of bullying and desire for good education, with low emphasis on science and technology. West *et al.* (1991) looked at factors associated both positively and negatively with schools and found that educational factors frequently emerged as being important — that the school should get good examination results, have good learning facilities, good facilities for practical work and so on. As for factors negatively associated with high schools, fear of bullying, gangs or violence, and travel problems or the school being too far away frequently emerged as important considerations.

The most significant issues cited in the literature seem to be of differing types, and perhaps fall under the following sorts of headings, some of which are much more ambiguous and difficult to interpret than others. First of all, there are clearly practical issues, such as ease of journey and/or access. Second are unambiguous organizational issues, such as size of school, single-sex schools and religious affiliations. Third, there are some issues that clearly relate to questions of social interaction, such as the child's own choice (or perhaps the parents deferring to the child's wishes), the child's existing friends or siblings. Fourth, are some organizational issues that are ambiguous in terms of how they are judged in practice, for instance, exam results, choice of subjects — are these issues part of the ways in which 'a good reputation' is discussed, or do parents sit down with different brochures and make detailed comparative assessments?

There are also some criteria that are very broadly expressed, for example, 'a good reputation', 'good relationships between staff and pupils', 'good discipline'. We also need to consider the question of the significance of *school climate* 'which may ultimately be the single most important criterion for both students and their parents' (Raywid, 1985, p. 446). Similarly, Hughes *et al.* (1990) found that active choice of primary school tended to be associated with an emphasis on 'school ethos'. Without more specification, these are extremely ambiguous in terms of what they actually mean — they can act as the sort of acceptable noises you make when giving reasons to others for your decision. What do these things actually mean, and how do parents judge them? How does this relate to the processes of decision-making discussed above? (For example, how are 'reputations' generated within specific networks of neighbours, friends and relatives?)

Finally, the issue of locality is also at present very ambiguous. Some studies seem to discuss placement at the local school as a 'non-choice', but how do parents actually evaluate the significance of proximity? For example, is it evaluated in terms of practical access (as mentioned above), of maintaining personal links, of wanting the child to be close to home? Do parents believe there are positive disadvantages in going to a non-local school? Throughout Europe, only small proportions of parents send their children to non-local schools (Macbeth, 1984). In England and Wales, Stillman and Maychell (1986) found that between 52 and 71 per cent of pupils in different areas went to the nearest school to their home. In Scotland in 1987/8, 10 per cent of parents of children at the stage of secondary school entry made requests for the child to be 'placed' at a school other than the one allocated (Echols *et al.*, 1990). At the primary school level, Hughes *et al.* (1990) found that while forty-three out of a total of 141 children had not been placed in the local school, with only fifteen of these children had the parents positively sought out a non-local school in the absence of negative features also being cited for the local school.

This study also found that placement at a non-local school was more likely to involve a complex decision-making process, with more than one school being considered. So there tends to be a situation of 'Will the local school do?' Proximity is even a significant issue for parents of children in private schools (Darling-Hammond *et al.*, 1985; Fox, 1985).

There are in any event different ways in which researchers categorize reasons given by parents which make analysis problematic. For instance, Stillman and Maychell (1986) draw upon Elliott *et al.*'s (1981) distinction between *process* and *product* reasons but regrouped their ninety-seven categories of reasons into four, namely process, product, geographic and unclassifiable. Yet there are significant difficulties about knowing where different categories of reasons should be placed within this scheme. West (1994) has put forward a different way of looking at factors raised by parents — namely whether the factors are 'structural', for example, a school being single-sex, small, close — or whether they are 'dynamic' such as 'good discipline'. She argues that for some parents structural factors are of overriding importance, while for others, dynamic factors are most important.

There is also the question of the patterns in the reasons given. Stillman and Maychell (1986) found 'no substantial differences between boys' and girls' parents' reasons . . . Indeed, for the most part the similarities in response rate were quite remarkable' (p. 83). More recent research carried out in London has found differences between parents from different ethnic or religious groups, parents with daughters and sons and so on. Suffice it to say that there appear to be differences between different types of parents with more parents of girls than boys preferring single-sex schools — at least in London — and with parents from some ethnic/religious groups rather than others preferring single-sex schools for their daughters (further discussion of these studies can be found in West, 1994).

Going back to the early study by Elliot (1981) once again, he found that mothers gave more emphasis than fathers to 'child's happiness at school', and 'opportunities for personal/social development'. This is an important finding for our own starting point in which we surmise that there are patterns both to the decision-making processes and to responsibilities taken — patterns on gender lines for the parents and the children. We turn now to look at how these various contexts and conceptual matters influenced our design of a study of parental choice.

Conclusions

In this introductory chapter we have presented the origins of our study and located it in a number of different contexts such as the social, political and policy oriented. We have also given some consideration to the range of conceptual issues and questions that have been raised in the broad literature on 'choice' of school amongst other things, issues that we consider necessary to address as a prelude to designing our study of parental choice of school. Our study was intended to explore 'family' diversity, and also to consider 'choice' processes more fully from the points of view of parents and children themselves. Furthermore, we regard the concept of 'choice' as problematic, as much the outcome of social interactions and processes as an act of rational judgment based on an objective and purposive search for relevant information. We turn our consideration now to the design of our research given the flavour of the questions about choice that we felt it necessary to address.

Note

1   The extent to which open enrollments lead to greater or lesser social segregation between schools is itself a complex issue, however. Where parental choice is defined within a particular programme designed to reduce social segregation, then it may help to promote such an objective. Thus, in the USA, open enrollment within certain predefined avenues has been seen at times to reduce the levels of segregation between schools, by allowing ethnic minority parents to send their children to out-of-area schools (Raywid, 1985).

Chapter 1

Choice of Research Design

Introduction

In this chapter we turn to a consideration of the issues about how to approach the study of parental choice of secondary school, given the questions that we have felt it necessary to raise. We consider the balance between quantitative and qualitative methods and the ways in which these impinged upon our design of our interviews and the selection of our samples. We also give a flavour of what our research design produced in terms of 'target' children and their parents.

Analysis Adopted: Quantitative and Qualitative Approaches

One of the aims of the project was to extend the methods used, to go beyond the highly structured and quantitative approaches taken by much of the existing literature. At the same time, the intention was to incorporate a mixture of methods. Within the history of social science research, there has been a predominant emphasis on the use of quantitative methods, which have been seen as providing greater scientific rigour. These methods may also have had a particular accord with the culture of western capitalism, with its emphasis on the importance of measurement and accurate counting. Social research was further enhanced in this direction by the advances in sampling and statistical theory and techniques that occurred around the time of the Second World War. While such advances may have led to some highly impressive outcomes, they may also at times have led social researchers to neglect theoretical and/ or sociological understanding for the sake of technical sophistication.

Substantive sociological concepts may thus have been shaped to fit the research methods rather than being driven by theoretical considerations. In particular, Bertaux (1991) argues that survey methods in social mobility studies have led to a neglect of those levels of sociological analysis that do not depend upon the study of individuals but involve an understanding of institutional and societal processes, including family interactions over time. The latter point has particular relevance to our own study.

By contrast, while qualitative methods have a long and respectable history within social research, their use and significance has remained more muted until recent years. Within the last twenty years, however, there has been an increasing interest in these methods, fuelled in particular, in sociology, by phenomenological theoretical developments and especially by the concerns of feminist researchers. This renewed and extended interest has led to the advent of new textbooks and specialist journals devoted to this approach to social research, such that quantitative methods can no longer be regarded as holding quite the pre-eminent position they once may have had (Brannen, 1992).

More recently still, however, there has been a new interest in research that seeks to combine the different approaches, along with methodological discussions about the possibilities in this direction (e.g. see Bryman, 1988; Brannen, 1992; Oakley, 1992; Reinharz, 1992). The term 'triangulation' is sometimes invoked, (in a looser sense than its original usage) to refer to the application of multiple methods within a single piece of social research.

Some writers, however, have suggested that the distinction between the different methods is itself illusory. Thus Oakley (1992) provides some compelling examples of the qualitative nature of quantification processes, and the often arbitrary quality of supposedly 'hard data'. Similarly, it is clear that much qualitative research incorporates elements of measurement and quantification. One of the major difficulties, however, in such discussion, is that it is not always clear upon what the distinction between qualitative and quantitative methods is based. Most directly, the distinction refers to differences in the form of data presented, in which case 'qualitative' seems simply to refer to 'the absence of quantification'. As Bryman (1988) points out, however, the distinction is multi-layered and complex, ranging from major philosophical and epistemological disputes, to fine technical discussions about the pros and cons of different methods. As Bryman elaborates, within this range there are further aspects of difference between quantitative and qualitative research, including the relationships that arise between researcher and 'subject', the researcher's stance in relation to the subject, the relationship between theory/concepts and research, the research strategy, the scope of the findings, and the image of social reality generated.

In the context of the present study, we had particular reasons for seeking to combine some elements of the different approaches to social research. We wanted to provide a rounded account despite some of the difficulties that arose in so doing. As mentioned before, much of the existing research in this area of parental choice has been highly structured and quantified. While this has enabled some broad generalizations to be made, the results are at times complex, ambiguous and difficult to interpret. The problem of interpretation is particularly exacerbated by a lack of information about what parents actually mean by the concepts they are using, for example, 'atmosphere', 'choice', 'discipline'. The other major problem is the common one within structured quantitative research, namely that a static cross-sectional picture emerges that is centred totally on individuals in isolation, with little understanding of underlying processes over time in the decision-making sequence, including the interactions that may occur between the different people concerned.

Research that seeks to combine different methods within one study may often do so by using a variety of methods at different stages or in different sites of the overall project (see examples reviewed by Bryman, 1988; or Reinharz, 1992). In the present research, resources only enabled the use of mixed research methods within one main research stage. Thus, within the constraints of the present study, the primary research tool has been that of the structured interview schedule, administered by interviewers to people selected from a prespecified sampling frame.

Within this overall method, the incorporation of a more qualitative approach was addressed by a number of means. First, an interest in process and in events over time led to the inclusion of questions specifically designed to investigate sequences in educational decision-making within the target child's life, and questions were also included about the parents' own educational histories and experiences. Second, open-ended questions were used at times in advance of more closed-ended questions on the same topic, enabling respondents to use their own language and speak from their own concerns before being given a checklist of prespecified items. Third, exploratory questions were also used to follow up on more closed-ended questions in order to gain more of a sense of how respondents understood key concepts used.

In practice, however, the issues encountered in actually seeking to combine qualitative and quantitative methods within one research tool led us to an awareness of a neglected topic within discussions of multi-methods research, that is the implications of the different methods for the power dynamics between researcher and researched. Ribbens has explored elsewhere (1989) some of the nuances of the ebb and flow of the research interview, and the implications of different styles of interviewing for the power balance between interviewer and interviewee, particularly in the light of feminist concerns with reciprocity and collaboration (Oakley, 1981; Davies, 1985). While she has argued that all researchers are in a position of power in constructing and interpreting the lives of others, it is clear that the ways in which this power is exercised differ quite markedly between different interviewing methods. The significance of this, within the present project, became apparent as the interviews progressed. The basic research tool was a long and detailed structured interview schedule which then set the tone of the encounter into that of an interviewer-led interaction. The person being interviewed is thus often appropriately described as a 'respondent', rather than an active participant. When more open-ended and exploratory questions were introduced, the power dynamics of the interaction were already established, and respondents did not generally shift into a more active and discursive style at these points. Yet at other times, it seemed that there were other stories to be told that were being muted within the confines of the structured interview, rather as Brown and Gilligan (1992) found that their structured traditional psychological research tools had the effect of silencing the voices of the girls to whom they wanted to listen.

It might be argued that this issue we found in resolving the different power implications of varying research methods occurred because we were limited to the one research tool and encounter. While this may certainly have sharpened the problem, we suggest that the overall dilemma is likely to remain in all research that seeks to combine both qualitative and quantitative methods. While *all* researchers do exercise power over their subjects of investigation, the timing and methods of doing so vary greatly between different research styles. In particular, structured methods always involve the early application of decision-making by the researcher, with prespecification of the research questions, concepts and variables in line with the interests and concerns of the researchers and their funders. This means that even if some portions of the research use more open-ended methods, this will always be done within an overall framework and agenda that has been laid down beforehand. Furthermore, where the qualitative data contradict the quantitative results, as Bryman points out, there may often be a tendency to assume the superiority of the quantitative material. In effect, this prioritizes the researcher's under-standings and interests over that of the researched. In other words, once the researcher has exerted power over the research in the form of prestructured and quantified methods, this power imbalance is only likely to be redressed with great difficulty in favour of the researched. Rist (1980) has coined the term 'blitzkrieg ethnography' to refer to structured research that claims to be ethnographic in ways that he disputes, particularly because the focuses of research are prespecified in such research rather than being allowed to develop over time, as in 'genuine' ethnography (discussed by Bryman, 1988).

The final difficulty we encountered in our own attempts to combine methods is a more mundane one, but is also commonly cited in discussions of multi-method research. It is the fact that the analysis of qualitative data is very time-consuming and tends to be neglected in favour of the more immediate possibilities of producing 'results' in a quantified format. Much of the potential of our more 'qualitative' data has as yet been left untapped.

Nonetheless, we do believe that our interest in multi-method research has been a great asset and produced dividends, particularly through the greater attention paid to process and to meaning. As we present our substantive discussion and 'findings' we will also explore further how far our multi-methods have enhanced each other, providing further food for thought and the basis for further research and developments in research methodologies.

Issues in the Research Design

Inevitably of course, given the exigencies of time and money, we could only select a relatively small group of parents and pupils with whom to explore the variety and complexity of issues that we considered were being raised by the policy debates, referred to above, and our interpretation of the relevant issues from the range of literature with which we were familiar. However, we took the decision to explore different family contexts and circumstances by means of looking at differences in ethnicity and/or race, and social class as well as changing family composition, culture and structure.

At this stage we chose only to look at parents of children in *state financed primary schools*, whether LEA county or voluntary-aided schools. Our decision was partly based upon our knowledge of the accessibility of such schools compared to those within the private sector and also the predicted familial and cultural diversity as well as the ability range of pupils which would not have been found in the private sector. At the time, we assumed that parental choice of secondary school would be a significant issue for the majority of parents within the state system.

The ERA 1988 had an important impact in London in that it abolished the Inner London Education Authority (ILEA) and created in its place thirteen inner London education authorities in each of the twelve London boroughs and the City of London. These processes of political and administrative change in London meant that the LEAs were given longer than those outside of London to develop their systems of local management of schools (LMS). We chose London advisedly, however. As we have mentioned above, London seemed to us to be a rich vein in terms of its variety and diversity. Moreover, half of the research team is based in the Centre for Educational Research at the London School of Economics, and were formerly part of the ILEA's Research and Statistics Branch and therefore had extremely good contacts with the new local education authorities and their schools.

This study explores parents' attitudes to these various changes and how they were being considered in the immediate aftermath of the 1988 ERA. The two inner London boroughs were chosen for their contrasting social and demographic characteristics given the demise of the ILEA. As we have noted above, we considered London sufficient to provide the variety and contrasts around families in terms of social class, ethnicity and family form and structure. However, both LEAs that we selected contained primary schools that were socially and racially or ethnically mixed and both secular and religious schools. Given the traditional state approach to coeducational primary schooling, we assumed that we would find an even gender balance amongst the children. We hoped, however, that this selection of inner London schools would produce a range of different family structures and forms.

We chose Camden because it is a local authority that has always been politically dominated by Labour. It also has a wide range of LEA-maintained (county) and voluntary-aided secondary schools including religious, co-educational and single sex ones.

By contrast, we chose Wandsworth because it was in the vanguard of the new Conservative boroughs in supporting a range of new secondary schools to facilitate the processes of parental choice. In particular, the Director of Education for Wandsworth, Donald Naismith, had been an especially vocal and eloquent exponent of the new Conservative philosophy and tried to create the most appropriate environment for its implementation, along with the

Table 1.1: Numbers of county and voluntary-aided schools in our sample by LEA

Type of state school	Camden	Wandsworth
County	1	2
Voluntary	2	1
Total	3	3

Education Committee of the London borough of Wandsworth. In a short space of time the idea of magnet schools for the borough had been created based upon the American concept (see, 1992 Kelly; Whitty *et al.*, 1993) with the development of a city technology college, sponsored by the company ADT, being encouraged. This proposal for magnet secondary schools led to a large number of county schools opting for grant-maintained status, while those remaining in the LEA have, in various ways, adopted the 'magnet' or 'special-ization' concept, including a further technology college. Moreover, the LEA also provides information about grant-maintained schools and private schools that offer places, through the government's assisted places scheme, in its bro-chure, for parents with children in the last year of primary school, about the range of secondary schools available in the borough.

With this range of secondary schools we chose the primary schools carefully to ensure that we might have a mixture of parents, some of whom might be considering these new types of school. The original intention was to approach two primary schools in each borough, contrasting families making an explicit religious choice of school with those making a choice of an LEA-maintained school, namely one voluntary-aided school and one county school in each LEA. However, because the numbers of pupils on roll at two schools were very much smaller than had been anticipated, two additional schools (one voluntary school in Camden and one county school in Wandsworth) were approached. A total of six schools (three in Camden and three in Wandsworth) were thus involved, as shown in Table 1.1.

Design of the Interview Schedule for Parents

Semi-structured interview schedules were devised to enable the complex areas and issues that we were investigating to be adequately covered in accordance with the mixture of methods that we had decided to use and have discussed above. In particular, we tried to address issues of both process and procedure with respect to the ways in which parents went about 'choosing' schools. We also were keen to address the questions that we raised at the end of the intro-duction about parental involvement and responsibility in the decision processes.

Part of the interview sought to establish some background information about the target child and her or his family structure and form, household, family changes and social and geographical mobility and so on. Details about the child's preschool and educational experiences to date and their place

Table 1.2: *Distribution of parents across the two boroughs by type of school*

Type of school	Camden Parents	Wandsworth Parents	Total
County	10	21	31
Voluntary	26	13	39
Total Parents	36	34	70

within the family history were also sought. Additional parts of the interview schedule focused on the process of choosing a secondary school — who had been involved and when, the role of the child in the process, sources of information used to assist the choice process, factors considered to be more or less important and so on. Details about parents' attitudes to schooling and political views were also included in the schedule. Finally, we requested background information about parental occupations, ethnic background and the education that the parents had received.

The Research Sample of Families Achieved

Overall, seventy interviews were successfully carried out, representing a response rate of 48 per cent (similar to that found by Edwards *et al.*, 1989). Parents were approached by letter and invited to be interviewed in their own homes or in school. In five of the schools, headteachers were asked to distribute letters to all the parents of children in Year 6 (aged 10 to 11) inviting them to be interviewed (either at home or at school). Parents were requested to return a slip, indicating their willingness to be involved, in a postage-paid envelope to the research team. In fact, very few parents actually returned slips (only 18 per cent), and therefore letters were sent by post to parents who had not replied asking them to return a slip if they did *not* want to be interviewed. Parents were again approached and this time many more agreed to be interviewed — a total of 50 per cent from these five schools were finally interviewed. The sixth school agreed to be involved in the study when it had become apparent that fewer parents than originally expected were likely to be interviewed. In this school, the headteacher arranged for letters to be sent to the Year 6 parents inviting them to be interviewed and to return a slip in a postage-paid envelope whether or not they were prepared to be involved. An additional twelve parents were thus interviewed. The total numbers of parents across the schools are shown in Table 1.2. This can also be expressed in terms of the types of school within each borough as can be seen in Table 1.3.

Parents who were volunteers and non-volunteers

Some differences emerged between parents who volunteered to be interviewed (that is, those who responded to the letters sent out) and those who were

Table 1.3: Distribution of parents of the target children across the county and voluntary-aided schools

	County	Voluntary
Camden A	10	
Camden B		25
Camden C		1
Wandsworth A		13
Wandsworth B	9	
Wandsworth C	12	

interviewed after telephone contact or other means. We assumed that our original sampling method might produce more parents who were enthusiastic about education and schools for their children than the ones that we had to press to respond. In other words, we predicted that our sample might be biased in the direction of parents who took an active interest in education and were themselves more involved in education. We felt that we might miss those who, for various reasons, could not or did not participate in schools. Moreover, there might be a gender or family structure difference in participation in education and in our interviews. Other researchers have found that women in particular are often hard-pressed as mothers and might find the interview an added difficulty (Edwards, 1990). There was, we found, a trend for more parents who volunteered to like the school(s) they were applying to because of favourable first impressions (35 versus 13 per cent). There was also a trend for more parents who did not volunteer to report that their child liked the facilities at their preferred school (36 versus 13 per cent). More parents who did not volunteer mentioned as an important factor their child wanting to go to the school concerned (21 versus 0 per cent). In other words, these latter parents tended to leave the issues to the children rather than their own active involvement. We also found by contrast, that significantly more parents who volunteered reported that the teachers/headteacher at the school were an important factor in their choice of school (29 versus 3 per cent). In other words, these parents were concerned generally about educational matters.

Design of the Questionnaire to Pupils

A questionnaire was also designed for use with pupils who were in their final year of primary school and included those who were target children in the parents' study. This questionnaire was structured and simpler than the interview schedule to which we have just referred above. It asked for details of their preferred school, the sorts of things that would make them want to go to a particular school, secondary schools they would not want to go to, their preferred type of secondary school (single-sex, mixed, religious) and links with, and information about, secondary schools.

The Achieved Sample of Primary School Pupils

Year 6 pupils from five (primary) schools — two in Camden and three in Wandsworth — filled in a questionnaire under the supervision of one of the researchers. Those pupils who were not present on that particular day filled out a questionnaire on their return to school under the supervision of their class teacher.

A total of 134 questionnaires were completed, a response rate of 92 per cent. Of the 134 questionnaires completed, 43 per cent were filled in by boys and 57 per cent by girls. Forty per cent of the pupils were in Camden schools and 60 per cent in Wandsworth schools. Altogether, 57 per cent of the children attended county schools and 43 per cent attended voluntary (church) schools. In slightly over half of the children (70), the parents had been interviewed by us about the process of choosing a secondary school.

Conclusions

In this chapter we have tried to give a flavour of our approach to the question of choice of school, from the point of view of parents and children, in terms of methodologies and designs. We have demonstrated that the research question is not a simple matter in terms of the concepts of choice, family and education. We have also alluded to the complexity of the question in terms of methodology and research approach and why we decided to approach the issues through a mixture of methods.

Finally, we have discussed the actual samples of parents and pupils around whom the rest of this analysis will be based. We will address the issues through the eyes and voices of seventy parents and their 'target' children and we will supplement this with the voices or words of 134 pupils, including our target children, all drawn from two inner London boroughs and six different state-financed primary schools, involving a mixture of LEA county and voluntary aided schools.

We turn now to a consideration of the various social characteristics of the sample of parents and the relation to the wider population of parents in London.

Chapter 2

Characteristics of the Children and Their Families

Introduction

In this chapter we shall explore the various social characteristics of the target children and their families. These characteristics are drawn from the meetings with the seventy parents whom we interviewed about how they went about choosing schools. (We will not discuss here the other sixty-four children who filled in the pupils' questionnaire.) As we have mentioned in Chapter 1, we selected the families by finding a target group of children in particular state schools in inner London. We selected schools to try to maximize the variety of family backgrounds, in terms of race and/or ethnicity, social class, religious affiliation and family structures in order to explore the complexity of the processes of choice. Although we had slightly more difficulty than we had anticipated in getting a sufficiently large sample to compare and contrast these various social characteristics (as we noted above, more schools had to be approached), we have obtained a fascinatingly mixed sample of families on all the criteria that we assumed would yield diversity.

We will start by discussing various social characteristics of the sample families and then move on to look in more detail at family forms/structures and backgrounds before moving on, in subsequent chapters, to a detailed discussion of the ways in which this sample of parents, in particular, approached the process of their children's transfer to secondary school.

We should note that the majority of parents were interviewed in their own homes but some parents chose to be interviewed at school rather than at home, and some needed to have an interpreter. We have not, however, looked at whether or not there are differences between the interviewees in terms of their social characteristics and the place of interview, given the small numbers. However, we might surmise that this might have at least a small effect, given evidence about this from other surveys and studies (Edwards, 1990; Oakley, 1992; Rubin, 1981).

Table 2.1: Members of families interviewed about the target child

Person(s) interviewed	Percentage (N = 70)
Mother	70
Father	14
Mother and Father	9
Mother and Partner	3
Grandmother/Sister/Stepmother	4

Social Characteristics of the Sample of Families

We will look at issues to do with family relationships, social class and race/ethnicity starting from the target child and comparing the sample with parents in the locality from which the schools were selected. Our selection procedure of schools and target children eventually yielded seventy interviews with at least one parent from the families of the target children. In other words, we interviewed parents of seventy target children, although the actual number of parents interviewed was somewhat greater, especially because the majority took place in the family home. However, we only interviewed more than one parent or family member in 12 per cent of the families.

Table 2.1 shows that our interviews were held with *women* (either alone or jointly) in the vast majority (86 per cent) of families. We interviewed *mothers* on their own only in 70 per cent of the families, and mothers with the father or her partner in another 12 per cent of the families, and other women, usually in a surrogate mother capacity, in 4 per cent of the interviews.

The two interviewers made notes on these interviewees and their family situations as well as the interview process; some examples of these are given below. In some of the interviews there were language difficulties and, as noted, an interpreter had to be found.

> This mum was very keen to be interviewed . . . The mother never stopped talking but the father although there . . . did not want to be involved and we in fact moved from the lounge to the kitchen so he could watch TV . . .

> Both parents were present but mum did most of the talking.

> Mum is Japanese . . . Mum was very charming . . . There were some language problems as although Mum's English was quite good I sometimes had to rephrase my questions or she had to attempt her answers a few times before she said what she wanted to say.

> Only the father came for the interview, not the mother, and the interview was in school. Interpreter used — a young lady helping in

the nursery at school who also lives in the same road as the family so knows them.

Did not reply to the initial letter. Quite willing to be interviewed when contacted . . . Child lives with the grandmother so it was her I interviewed, in school.

Mother agreed to be interviewed in school.

Did not reply to initial letter . . . Spoke to daughter who said parents do not speak English but I could go when she would be there to interpret. Daughter is . . . at college. When I went I just saw her, not the parents. She has responsibility for dealing with everything for the younger members of the family . . . I think she represented her parents' views.

In this family, the wife agreed to be interviewed but when I got to the house the father was actually present to be interviewed and it seemed the wife did not actually live in the house.

This father particularly wanted to be the interviewee, even though it was his wife who was described as the main agent in making the choice of school. I think he was interested for professional reasons, since he was a secondary school teacher.

The stepmother took responsibility for answering during most of this interview, even though the father was present, until it got to the political questions, and then she turned to him to answer.

This mother was an early volunteer to our sample . . . a white working-class woman . . . who lived in a council flat.

Mrs X was interviewed at school . . . an early volunteer.

This mother talked to me in the kitchen, a warm and humorously emotional woman who expressed very strong feelings and anxieties about her son's education, and she hugged me when I left.

It is important to note at this juncture that we did achieve a diverse sample of families, as can be gleaned from the above comments, especially in terms of family-household structures and this is shown in Table 2.2. This shows that just over half of the target children lived with both parents (59 per cent)

Table 2.2:   The target children's households

Child lives with . . .	Percentage of children (N = 70)
Mother and father	59
Mother alone	23
Mother and partner	11
Father alone	3
Father and partner	1
Other	3

Table 2.3:   Distribution of children across county and voluntary primary schools

School type	Camden	Wandsworth	Total (%)
County	10	21	31 (44)
Voluntary	26	13	39 (56)
Total	36	34	70 (100)

while almost a quarter of our sample lived only with their mothers rather than in two-parent households.

We had expected to interview mothers rather than fathers in the majority of cases, given that it is well-known that they have the main family responsibilities for schooling and education (David, 1993) and also that they are generally the interviewees in research studies in relation to children (David *et al.*, 1993; Brannen, 1992; Oakley, 1992; Edwards *et al.*, 1989; West, 1992a). Moreover, we had predicted that the changes in family structure and form would produce a sizeable number of lone parent families and as we have just noted almost a quarter of the target children lived in such households.

These families also did not come in equal proportions from the six schools that we had selected. Indeed, the numbers of interviewee parents ranged from one to twenty-five in each school. Nevertheless, we found that we had quite an evenly mixed picture with respect to the *type* of school from which the families of the target children came — altogether, 56 per cent of the parents had children in county schools and 44 per cent had children in voluntary (church) schools. Overall, we also had a relative 'balance' of parents/families from Camden and Wandsworth (51 per cent versus 49 per cent). It is, however, interesting to note that just over a quarter (28 per cent) of the children in our Camden schools were in county schools, compared with nearly two-thirds (62 per cent) of the children in our Wandsworth schools, as shown in Table 2.3. We also found that the distribution of family relationships was relatively balanced across the two boroughs with no significant differences between the number of children living with their mothers and fathers, with their mothers alone, with their mothers and her partner or in other family situations. In fact, in relation to the number of children living with their father alone, there was only one such family in each borough.

Gender of the Target Children

Given our selection of coeducational primary schools, albeit that they varied in terms of their secular or religious status, we hoped to achieve a gender balance in terms of the target children. This turned out to be very successful and we had relatively equal proportions of boys and girls in the sample of families. The target child was a boy in just over half the cases (51 per cent) and a girl in just under half (49 per cent); in other words, there were 36 boys and 34 girls whose parents we interviewed.

Social Class and Our Analysis

This is a study that seeks to disentangle 'family' processes, to elucidate the parts played by the different individuals within the family/household during the child's transfer into secondary education. We have thus sought to highlight mothers, fathers, children and other significant individuals as separate social actors each with their own perspective and input into the transfer process. Yet, when it comes to the analysis of social class patterns in our data, we are faced with the key difficulty that social class is normally assigned to the family/ household as a unit, rather than to the individuals within it. This situation has led to detailed, lengthy and heated debates in relation to the social class classification of women in particular (Goldthorpe, 1982; Stanworth, 1984). There are also, however, further issues to consider in relation to the social class position of children, especially with regard to their educational experiences.

The central dilemma is that it is clear that household membership does make a difference to people's lives in a variety of ways, so there are good reasons at times not to adopt an individualistic approach to social class classification. Yet the traditional method has been to assign the household to a particular class classification by reference to the single indicator of the occupation of head of household (generally, of course, male). This approach clearly raises great difficulties about the theoretical and empirical adequacy of such a measure for the description and explanation of the lives of women and children. How are we to interpret the information from one generation to the next? In other words, can parents' social class be used to understand children's development and education? Some significant studies of the lives of children have found that it is only through the use of a multidimensional approach to social class classification that they can find a satisfactory measure. Such multi-dimensional classification systems tend to incorporate factors related to the mother's life as well as the father's (e.g. her class of origin, or her educational qualifications), as well as factors that impinge directly on the life of the child, such as housing (Douglas *et al.*, 1967; Osborn and Morris, 1979).

The traditional approach, based on the occupations of fathers rather than mothers, also clearly raises difficulties in situations of changing household formations. Given the clear evidence of family change and family diversity, not all fathers now live with their children. This makes the social class attribution of lone parent families particularly difficult. The social class of mothers itself poses analytical problems and cannot generally be simply substituted for that of fathers. Thus there is the difficulty of comparing social class positions across diverse family-households and structures.

These difficulties and dilemmas about social class continue to perplex researchers and theorists alike. In the absence of any wider consensus, we clearly had to make some decisions that would be both practical and relevant to our own study. In the event, we have based our measure on two key decisions: first, we used occupation as our basis for classification; second, we have carried out analyses using both father's and mother's occupation.

'No rival to occupation as the basis of social class has ever really reared its head in Britain' (Marsh, 1986, p. 1). It is not surprising that 'occupation' has remained, since its first systematic use at the turn of the century, the single most used variable in the measurement of social position. In the first place, it correlates more widely than any other single measure with many other aspects and elements of social stratification, such as family background, education, income, social standing, lifestyle etc. Second, it is an accurate predictor of many other social variables, such as morbidity and mortality rates. However, it may not be as useful as a predictor across the generations, a point that we will discuss in more depth below. Third, it is a comparatively easy measure to collect, partly, perhaps, because we (in general) have become used to being asked, and very few people object to giving details of their work and occupation. Fourth, it is generally recognized to be the major determining characteristic behind social position. Indeed, when asked what characteristics they would use to describe middle-class and working-class people, around two-thirds mentioned 'occupation' (Kahan *et al.*, 1966).

It is, therefore, unlikely that any better single-variable index can be found for general routine usage as a measure of social position than 'occupation' and its derivatives (although note the use of multi-dimensional indices referred to above). There are, however, some further considerations with regard to the use of occupation for this purpose. First, how best is occupation to be recorded and what additional supplementary details (full/part time, past/present, etc.) should be collected with it, and second, in what ways should the information, once collected, be interpreted and used?

Many of the schemes fail because they do take a normative position on occupations on the assumption of no gender or ethnic differences in the relationship to or involvement in the labour market. This is the case especially when they are used to classify women's occupations, or the occupations of different ethnic groups, since they tend to lump together many such individuals into a few low-status occupational categories. There are several additional problems with many commonly-used scales when used to classify women's occupations. First, not all women are involved in paid employment and this is particularly true when they have children and very young or even school-age children. Second, the distinction between manual and non-manual work — a feature of many classification systems — is difficult to apply to some occupations as it involves various types of 'people servicing work'. In addition, women who are self-employed tend to work part-time and have few employees — their status and therefore their position in the labour market is thus different from that of self-employed men. (Heath and Britten, 1984, also argue for women office workers and shop workers to be classified separately.)

A third crucial issue underlying any discussion of women's social class is that men and women occupy distinct sections of the labour market (see Arber *et al.*, 1986; Marshall *et al.*, 1988). The Registrar General's Social Classes and Socio-Economic Groups were constructed on *a priori* grounds for men. Goldthorpe's classes and the Hope-Goldthorpe and Cambridge scales also focused on men. There are a number of reasons why it is problematic to use classifications developed for one section of the population (men) for another (women). Occupational Unit Groups (OUGs) — the basis of most occupational classifications — provide less differentiation for women's than men's occupations; for example, 52 per cent of women are concentrated in only five of the 223 OUGs (Dale *et al.*, 1983) and nearly a quarter of all women working full-time are classified in one OUG (clerks and cashiers) compared with 5 per cent of men. Similarly, nurses of all levels from untrained nursing auxiliaries to Chief Nursing Officers are coded in the same OUG but have very different pay and promotion prospects.

Research studies on parental choice, carried out in the Inner London Education Authority (ILEA) Research and Statistics Branch before its abolition, used a simplified form of the Registrar General's classification rather than any more complex measure using a combination of variables (e.g. occupation, housing, education) (West *et al.*, 1984; West and Varlaam, 1991; Hunter, 1991). This was because London-wide data were available on parental occupations. Biennially, the Research and Statistics Branch carried out a survey of pupils in the ILEA's schools (the Education Priority Index survey) in order to assist with the allocation of resources to schools. As part of this exercise, teachers were asked to provide details of both parents' occupations when the child was living with both parents. Where there was a lone parent household, the partner was coded as absent. The fact that these London-wide data were available meant, in practice, that it was desirable to collect comparable data for small-scale surveys to enable comparisons to be made between samples selected for research studies — including those on parental choice — to be compared with the total population thus allowing one to establish whether or not the sample under investigation was representative of the population from which it is drawn.

Both West and Varlaam (1991) and Hunter (1991) collected equivalent information to enable samples obtained to be compared with the population in the ILEA in terms of their social class make-up and found their samples broadly comparable. A further study by West (1992a) also collected information on parental occupations and the resulting data established that the samples under investigation were atypical in terms of the parents' social background.

Table 2.4: Social background characteristics of mothers and fathers in our sample

Social background	Father*	Mother*
Non-manual	43	71
Skilled manual	31	7
Semi-skilled/unskilled	11	7
Economically inactive	1	16
Unknown	12	0

Note: * Percentages do not add up to 100 because of rounding.

Particularly where samples are to some extent self-selected (as in many interview studies of parents), it is important to establish whether or not they are systematically different from the parents of the whole school population. Differences between the samples may have implications for the interpretation of the results obtained, and, as such, data on parental occupation are worth collecting even if the measures are not perfect. There are, as we have noted, problems with using this social classification system and in this study we made comparisons between groups of parents using both father's social class and mother's social class background. The latter takes on board criticisms made by Heath and Britten (1984) about the measurement of women's social class and is more discriminatory in that it has a category of non-manual office workers and a category of non-manual shop workers and others.

For our purposes we have decided to use both mother's and father's social class separately to illustrate the difficulties of being able to attribute social class on the basis of occupation. In the process of interviews with the seventy families, we tried to establish some measure of social class by questions about the occupations and employment status of the parents involved in the interviews. For our analysis, we looked at mothers' and fathers' social backgrounds separately. Moreover, to try and get a more accurate picture, we used the mother's previous occupation to determine the social class if she was not currently in paid employment. This yielded the information given in Table 2.4. What is particularly interesting is that the mothers' social class backgrounds were generally in occupations that were 'higher' than those of the fathers. This is not surprising in the light of the above discussion, and is largely accounted for by a high percentage of mothers (34 per cent) in, or having previously worked in, non-manual office work.

Although we were keen to examine how mothers' and fathers' occupational backgrounds differed, we were also keen to establish how our sample of parents resembled the parents of primary school pupils in the two London boroughs. To do this we made direct comparisons with the Inner London Education Authority's Education Priority Index (ILEA, 1989). This entailed using *current* occupation and employment status to produce a combined parental occupation variable. This required us to use the father's occupation, but where the father was either *unemployed* or *absent*, we replaced it with the mother's occupation.

Table 2.5: Occupational background characteristics of our parent sample and primary school parents in the two boroughs

Social Background	Percent of Parents in Sample	Percent of Parents in Camden	Percent of Parents in Wandsworth
Non-manual	47	31	30
Skilled manual	21	18	24
Semi-skilled/unskilled	6	23	21
No wage earner	17	23	20
Unknown occupation	9	5	5
Parents absent	0	1	1

Note: Percentages do not add up to 100 because of rounding.

This yielded the data in Table 2.5, which we have presented in comparison with that of the overall parental occupational background of primary school parents in the two boroughs. We can see from it that our sample of parents was not representative of parents in the two boroughs in terms of parental occupations. A higher proportion of the parents in our sample were in non-manual occupations than in the two boroughs as a whole. Although there was a similar proportion of parents in skilled manual occupations, far fewer were in semi-skilled or unskilled occupations. The proportions of parents in the other occupational categories were not markedly different. Our sample of parents, using this particular method, therefore was revealed as being predominantly middle-class and skilled working-class. In other words, the semi-skilled and unskilled manual workers and the unemployed are underrepresented in the study and we have what might be considered a 'mainstream' sample of parents in terms of social class. This has important implications for the interpretation of our findings that will be discussed further in later chapters.

Race/Ethnicity of our 'Parent Sample'

We were also interested to establish the racial and/or ethnic characteristics of the families that we interviewed. In order to do this we asked the interviewee for her/his ethnic background and also for that of the father of the target child. We then combined this information to produce the child's ethnicity (Table 2.6).

In very bald terms our sample of pupils' families is somewhat less heterogeneous than the primary school pupils in Camden and Wandsworth, derived from the teachers' identification of the pupils' ethnicities (provided for the ILEA's Educational Priority Index). In both Camden and Wandsworth overall, as can be seen in Table 2.7, only slightly more than half (50 per cent) of the primary school pupils were reported to be white and from English, Scottish, Welsh or Irish backgrounds. In Camden, a quarter of the pupils were either Asian or Afro-Caribbean and in Wandsworth almost a third of the pupils were in these categories.

Table 2.6: Race/ethnic characteristics of the target children

Ethnic background	Percentage of children (N = 70)
White	71
Black — African	1
Black — Caribbean	6
Black — Other	6
Indian	6
Pakistani	3
Bangladeshi	3
Chinese	1
Other	3

Table 2.7: Race/ethnic characteristics of pupils in the two boroughs (ILEA, 1989)

Ethnicity/Race	Wandsworth	Camden
Afro-Caribbean	21	8
English, Scottish, Welsh, Irish	54	55
Asian	10	17
Others	15	20

The differences between the ethnicities/races of our sample and the population of the boroughs as a whole may have to do with the ways in which people from minority ethnic or racial backgrounds understand and/or perceive interviews such as we carried out, and choose whether or not to be involved. Edwards has discussed these issues in relation to her studies of mature women students (Edwards, 1990; 1993).

The interviewers also made notes about the various families that they met as an *aide-mémoire.* Their sketches of the families also flesh out the racial and ethnic diversity of our sample of parents. We offer the following from their thumbnail sketches:

Bangladeshi parents feel very cut off from education here as they cannot communicate with anyone themselves in English;

He is Scottish but his wife is Anglo-Indian;

She was Jewish, married to someone from Trinidad;

Swiss mother married to Irish father;

Father was in the Army and lives in Germany and there is no longer any contact with him;

Family are from Northern Ireland;

Mother was Jewish married to a Roman Catholic;

Mum is Japanese, Dad is Greek;

A Portuguese couple;

This was a Scottish mum married to a German dad;

This Indian mother . . . had left her husband after domestic violence and had been homeless for a time;

A black Caribbean woman . . . she gave very little information about her son's father.

Characteristics of the Families/Households of the Target Children

In the above introductory section we mentioned that almost a quarter of the target children came from lone mother households and less than two-thirds (59 per cent) came from mother and father households, although if we add in the number of children living with their mother and her partner, well over two-thirds of the sample lived in a 'two-parent' household.

In other words, in 41 per cent of the families, the target child was not living with both their natural parents as in a 'traditional nuclear family'. Of the 41 per cent of children who lived in such non-traditional family situations, just over one-third (34 per cent) regularly (or occasionally) spent nights with their other parent and/or partner. Overall, there were no marked differences between the households in which girls and boys lived, with one notable exception — namely that in all three cases where the child lived with the father alone or with the father and partner, the children were boys as opposed to girls.

As we indicated above, the majority of the family-households of the target children were white but there were a number of target children who were either black or Asian. The family structures did not differ significantly — over half of the white families were traditional compared with over two-fifths (four out of nine) of the black families and over two-thirds of the Asian families (seven out of nine). These findings are not in line with other research and point again to the atypical nature of the sample of parents that we interviewed. In other studies, such as Mirza (1992), there tend to be stronger differences in family form or structure between certain racial or ethnic minorities.

We also give some consideration to variations in terms of family size. The number of children in the households in our sample of families ranged from one to seven. In only 16 per cent of families was the target child an only child. As we might have expected, given recent population trends and trends in the birth rate, over half of all the families were quite small with almost 60 per cent in families of only one or two children, and almost a quarter in families with three children. In nearly one in five families (19 per cent) there were four or more children.

We had expected to find a variety of family forms, including reconstituted families or families with stepparents and/or stepchildren. Indeed, we found that in 17 per cent of the families, the target child lived with half-siblings (with or without siblings).

We also found a large proportion of families in which the target child was the eldest or only child — 44 per cent. We had wanted to look at the types of schools attended by older siblings as a way of getting at the complex processes of choosing schools for the target child. Questioning about the type of school(s) attended by older siblings was therefore only applicable for thirty-nine of the target children (but for two of them no information was available). The siblings of these thirty-seven children attended various types of schools: 78 per cent were in county or voluntary schools; 3 per cent were in private schools and 5 per cent in grant-maintained schools; 14 per cent had been to other types of school or a mixture of different types of schools.

We will return to discuss these issues in greater depth in Chapter 7 as part of looking at the kinds of social factors and relationships that families take into account in the process of deciding upon schools. Suffice it here to say that we have indeed found a very complex sample of families in terms of household structures and relationships, which is as we had originally predicted, and these varieties of households will inform our detailed analysis.

The Target Child's Early Life and Education

We were also interested in establishing the continuity or change in family-households over the target child's lifetime as a measure of the significance of these family patterns in the child's and the parents' lives. The parents interviewed were asked whether their child had lived with the same adults since she or he was born. In less than two-thirds (60 per cent) of the households the child had lived with the same adults, while 7 per cent had lived 'mostly' with both parents. Fourteen per cent had always lived with the mother and 6 per cent always with the father. In 13 per cent of the families, there had been more than one change in the child's household, quite a large proportion given the varied characteristics of the families to which we have just referred, although it seems that the mother (as we might have expected) is the relatively constant person with whom the child lives. Just over a quarter of the interviewees indicated that they had lived in the same house/flat since their child was born. For those who had *not* lived at the same address (N = 51) nearly one-fifth (18 per cent) reported that their child's schooling was something that they had considered when moving.

We were also interested in the child's educational development and so parents were asked whether or not the target child had been to any preschool

Table 2.8: Types of preschool groups attended by the target children

PreSchool	Percentage of Children* [N = 61]
Nursery class (state)	47
Playgroup	26
Mother and toddler group	17
Social services day nursery	14
Nursery school (state)	9
Nursery school (private)	9
Other	3

Note: * Percentages add up to more than 100, as children frequently attended more than one preschool group.

groups before starting school and, if so, what sort of group had been attended. The vast majority of children (87 per cent) had been to at least one preschool group. This chimes in with other evidence about the fact that the majority of preschool children now do have some out-of-home and collective or group care and/or education before the start of compulsory schooling (New and David, 1985; Cohen and Fraser, 1993). This is also important for considering the kinds of issues that the parents bring to bear on a child's education and social development.

Bronwen Cohen (1988) shows that in 1985 there was preschool provision available in the UK for 39 per cent of the population aged 0–4 in a range of facilities from LEA nursery schools or classes to day nurseries to child-minders. However, this probably overestimates the numbers of children catered for by these facilities, since some children might attend more than one. The year 1985 is relevant to our data in that in this year our sample children would have been 3 or 4 years old. Table 2.8 shows the types of preschool groups that the young children attended. Peter Moss's figures (1990) show the number of places in publicly funded childcare services as a percentage of all children in the age group. In the UK in 1988, there were places for only 2 per cent of under-3s and places for 35–40 per cent of age three to compulsory school age children. This figure matches our sample data somewhat better than that of Cohen's.

We also wanted to establish continuity and change in the target child's relationships, not only in the family-household, but also in their educational settings. This is particularly relevant in the light of our finding (discussed later) about the numbers of children who move into secondary school as part of a group of their primary school and neighbourhood friends and peers. Parents were therefore asked whether their child moved with any children from their most recent preschool group to infant school. Over three-quarters reported that they had, about one-fifth (21 per cent) had moved with one or two children and over a half (56 per cent) had moved with several children. When asked whether their child had attended any other schools apart from the one she or he was currently attending, just under one-fifth (19 per cent, or 13 children) reported that she or he had. The school was a local school in five families, more than one local school in two families, one distant school in five families and a combination in one case. Four children moved from this school to their current school with other children and in all cases, these were siblings.

Conclusions

We have tried to show how our sample of families is a varied and heterogeneous one in terms of the class, ethnicity, race and gender mix. We have also shown that the family form and composition does indeed reflect the varied nature of family life in Britain today, albeit not statistically representative of the situation in inner London at least in relation to class and ethnicity/race. The sample is also not representative of the country as a whole in terms of household structures; nationally, 19 per cent of households with dependent children are lone parent (so the percentage of children living in lone parent households will be even lower, given that lone parent families tend to be smaller). In addition, national figures show rather more children than in our sample live with a married couple; nationally the figure is 85 per cent (Central Statistical Office, 1992).

Far from it being the case that the vast majority of children live in traditional nuclear families, in which the parents are the 'natural' parents and also are married to each other, our sample illustrates the variety of different patterns that exist. Of course, it is too small to get at the really subtle differences in family form in terms of marriage and cohabitation and thereby the details of biological parenthood. However, we can show that the 'Kelloggs cornflake packet' image of the white, middle-class, two-parent two-children (boy and girl) pattern is far from the complex reality (see New and David, 1985, for a further discussion of this). It exists only for the minority of our sample and we have found very interesting variations on that pattern and theme. We have also found that mothers' involvement with their children's rearing *is* the relatively constant theme, despite the range and variety of backgrounds, households and patterns. What is also remarkable at this stage is the fact that far from it being the *norm* that children stay at home with their mothers in the preschool years, whether or not the mothers are involved in employment, the vast majority of children now attend some out-of-home care and/or education. This may, in fact, have a significant impact on subsequent schooling and thinking about the processes of schooling. We turn now to look at how these varied patterns of family life relate to decisions about children's schooling.

Chapter 3

Who Makes the Choice — Mothers, Fathers, Children or All Together?

Introduction

In this chapter we shall look at the families in our sample from the point of view of their interactions and relationships in terms of making decisions about the children's education. We were interested in how different families in varied contexts went about the process of making decisions and who was involved in the various processes. We were especially concerned to look at whether different types of families — in terms of social class, ethnicity/race and family structures — used different procedures from each other in these processes. As far as we are aware this is not something that has been looked at carefully by other researchers in the field. Elliott (1981, 1982) is the only researcher to consider differences between mothers and fathers but he is more concerned about their differences over the content of the decision — what he calls 'process' versus 'product' factors — rather than what we consider to be the complex social processes leading up to the 'final decision' on choice of secondary school.

Of course, it is also important to consider whether or not this particular issue of secondary school choice was of salience to any of the families and then in what kinds of ways. It could, of course, be the case that the question of 'choice' of secondary school is not seen as of particular importance or as a major decision to parents at all, despite all the rhetoric about parental choice. It could be that some if not all families, despite all the evidence about family changes and family diversity, regard this issue of 'making a decision' as part of the extension of mothers' child care responsibilities. On the other hand, particular families such as lone parent families or families from particular racial minorities may have a special approach to such questions. It is how this responsibility for family decision-making is interpreted that is the essence of this chapter.

Parents' Taking the Main Responsibility

We start by looking at our findings on who took the main responsibility in the family for deciding on their children's education, and particularly the secondary school to which the target child should go. Indeed, our starting point was to look at the ways in which responsibilities for educational decisions were taken in varied family settings. We were particularly interested in whether or not changes in decisions within specific family forms or structures are made in different ways from those in other families in relation to education. We were equally interested in whether or not changes in educational policies towards consumerism and markets had affected how families make decisions, especially about schools. We wanted to be able to put together these parallel changes in family life and educational policy to develop a picture of the processes of 'choice'.

We were, however, most concerned about whether or not these changes, in the broader contexts of family life and educational policy, had altered the ways in which responsibilities for educational decisions were viewed and taken. As we have noted before, responsibility for child-rearing has usually been seen as the main responsibility of mothers rather than fathers. However, little is known about whether particular decisions in relation to a child's education are taken by mothers, fathers or some combination of both.

It certainly seems to be the case that mothers are expected to be entirely responsible for a child's development before the age of compulsory schooling, especially in terms of health and daily child care. At primary school, mothers are expected first to ensure their child's adequate preparation and daily attendance and second to 'help' with aspects of school work. Elsewhere, both separately and together, Ribbens and David have discussed these rather complex, issues (see for example David *et al.*, 1993; David, 1993).

Rather less is known about taking the 'main' educational decisions such as choice of primary and/or secondary school, although Ribbens has explored the little evidence that there is for this (Ribbens, in David *et al.*, 1993, ch. 3). In the situation where family relationships are changing would the responsibilities be the same between mothers and fathers, or would mothers in lone parent families have more responsibility? And how would the children in varied family settings become involved in the processes of decision-making? Would changes in families and educational policies have an impact upon how families felt about taking responsibility for this educational decision?

Ribbens, for example, has written about how these responsibilities are divided up, with respect to child care in the early years, from her study of mothers with a child aged 7. She argues that:

> The position of fathers in relation to this boundary of mother–child responsibility is a rather ambiguous one, since paternal involvement may be felt to be supportive or threatening by mothers. If childcare is one of the very few areas in which women may potentially experience a sense of authority, they may be very wary of relinquishing this too easily . . . Women's variable expectations towards maternal employment and paternal involvement in childcare may relate to class differences between women in the likely equation of any ensuing potential costs

and benefits that may accrue to them . . . What does seem to be clear, however, is that increasing rates of maternal employment in industrialised societies do not seem to be changing the underlying pattern of *maternal responsibility and authority* within families. Even where both parents are in full-time paid employment, alternative childcare is still largely seen as the responsibility of the mother both to arrange and pay for. (p. 65, 70–1)

Ribbens then goes on to argue that: 'Maternal responsibilities may indeed at times constitute an overwhelming burden, but they may also at times provide a welcome and novel experience for the exercise of *authority* as women' (p. 74).

She reviews how the mothers in her study sample had 'chosen' the primary schools for their children alongside the evidence of the few other studies concerning choice of primary school. She argues that the other studies have rarely differentiated mothers' views on school choice from fathers' preferences. She writes:

Within the state system, most of the women in my study felt that they did have some choice of school for their child, and for many this represented the most *powerful point of contact* with a school, when they might be able to seek any continuity they expected between home and school values. Choice of school was also the point at which fathers were most likely to be involved in decision-making and contact with the school, e.g. in visiting schools formally before putting a child's name down. Occasionally there might be an outright conflict of ideas between mother and father on the subject, which might be resolved in either the mother's or the father's favour. Some men, however, were described as leaving such decisions entirely up to the women. *Even where a father was involved in the decision, the mother might have paved the way for this, by making some initial investigations of her own . . .*

It is very notable that studies concerned with parental choice of school have not so far paid any attention to the question of *which* parent takes the primary role in this decision, or *how mothers, fathers and children negotiate the decision between them.* (p. 80–1, our emphasis)

This is a gap we aim to fill by looking here at how the *main responsibility* was negotiated in a variety of different family settings. In this study we started the process by asking the parents in the interviews, whom, as we have already noted in the previous chapter, were largely the mothers, who they felt had the main responsibility for deciding on the secondary school for the target child. Given that the main interviewee was the mother, and our prior knowledge of the research literature on this subject, we rather assumed that it would be, in

Table 3.1: Main responsibility for choosing school

Main responsibility	Percentage of parents (N = 70)
Mother	46
Both parents	20
Both parents and child	11
Father	7
Child	7
Mother and child	4
Other	4

Note: Percentages do not add up to 100 because of rounding.

the majority of situations, the mother. The initial responses of the interviewees to this issue of who had the main responsibility are shown in Table 3.1.

In nearly half of the families whom we interviewed, the mother was felt to have had the main responsibility for deciding to which school the child should go. This confirms the finding that David *et al.* made in the above cited study of mothers of young children going to primary school. Ribbens wrote:

> Most of the mothers in my own study did express a sense of having exerted some control over which schools their children attended. Yet in line with other studies of primary school choice, very few . . . used this influence by reference to 'educational' considerations . . . almost all mothers believe that 'education' in the school system is a 'good thing' and many may feel a sense of relief at being relieved of responsibility for their children for substantial portions of time . . . (p. 88–9)

Although our findings are in accordance with those of Ribbens', there is a major difference in the two studies, in that we are here concerned with choice of *secondary* rather than primary school. However, as we have noted, there are no studies that have looked explicitly at the gender differences in parental choice of secondary school nor at the changing context.

In one-fifth of the families in this study *both* parents were reported to have had the main responsibility and in just over 10 per cent of the families, both parents and the child were felt to have had the main responsibility. This broad pattern was found in both the London boroughs. Interestingly, however, the children themselves were the ones with the main responsibility in Camden in 14 per cent of the cases (five children), by contrast with Wandsworth, where the child alone never had the main responsibility. In addition, in Camden, in three cases the child and mother were reported to have had the main responsibility together, a situation that was not reported at all in Wandsworth.

If we examine who the various participants in the decision-making process are (see Table 3.1), and add together the percentages which include mothers, we find that mothers were said to have had the main responsibility in 81 per cent of the families whereas, adding up the percentages which include fathers, fathers were only involved in less than half that, namely 38 per cent of the families. Children on aggregate were only seen to be involved with the main responsibility in 22 per cent of the families. This then does confirm our feeling that mothers tended to take part in the main responsibility in the vast majority of situations. Perhaps even more significantly, children were seen as part of the main responsibility in almost a quarter of the families.

Of course, it is important to consider what these various interviewees understood by the phrase 'main responsibility', given these varied answers. The women interviewees might have felt that they 'prepared the ground' for the decision which was then taken in consultation with other family members, including the target child themselves, as we have already noted with respect to primary school decisions. Moreover, having the main responsibility might be seen by the parents to be an obligation rather than a right. In other words, the parents could have felt that it was their responsibility to decide, given the age of the child and the awesome nature of such a decision. We will look further into this matter below. It has certainly been viewed as a major moral dilemma to consider the appropriate age of majority for adolescents — what is sometimes known as Gillick competence after the major legal decision about the age of responsibility for contraceptive decisions for girls (David, 1986). Clearly here we are getting at contesting definitions of what parents and children may mean by responsibility and whether or not this question of secondary school choice is a key issue for responsibility.

The Influence of Gender and/or Race on the Main Responsibility for Choice

There were no marked differences between parents in the two different parts of London in which we carried out our study. Moreover, there were very few differences over the main responsibility for choosing a school in terms of the sex of the child. In other words, the mother remained the main person responsible whether it was for a son or a daughter. The only slight differences were that where the father had the main responsibility, it was more often in relation to a son than to a daughter (11 versus 3 per cent) and where the child was felt to have had the main responsibility, it was more often in connection with a girl than a boy (12 versus 3 per cent). This is indeed interesting in relation to our above comments about when boys and girls as adolescents are thought to reach 'maturity' and are capable of making their own decisions over aspects of their lives.

Some of the comments made by parents show how different participants are involved in the decision. In one family a father from Pakistan made the decision for his son who 'was abroad with his mother at the time'. In another family, also a two parent household, a mother said: 'My daughters always decide. I don't decide. I try to decide'. Indeed she mentioned that her child

Table 3.2: *Family structures by participants in the main responsibility*

Main responsibility includes:	Percentage of ...		
	Mother and father families (N = 41)	**Lone mother families (N = 16)**	**Others (N = 13)**
Mother	80	100	62
Father	46	19	38
Child	32	13	8

had had the main responsibility. In another family, in which the grandmother was interviewed, it was said that the main responsibility was jointly between 'the grandmother, mother and daughter' and that the final decision was the daughter's.

In terms of race and/or ethnicity, there were no clear-cut differences, which is not surprising given the small numbers of black and Asian parents in the study.

Main Responsibility for Choice by Family Relationships and Social Background

As we noted above, we assumed from the limited research evidence that the main responsibility for deciding upon a secondary school would be taken by the mother, whatever the family situation, given her general responsibilities for child care and child rearing. Interestingly, however, the main responsibility for the decision on the secondary school did not necessarily link the responsibility with the different family structures. In other words, it was *not* invariably the case that in lone mother households the mother alone had the main responsibility. Although this was the case in three-quarters of such lone mother households (twelve out of sixteen), in the remaining four cases, it was the mother and father who had the main responsibility (two), the child and both parents (one) or the child and the mother (one). In other words, lone mother families in our sample do not have *sole* responsibility for the decisions about schooling, despite the fact that such mothers do have the *main* responsibility for looking after the child(ren). It is also interesting to note that one of the lone fathers reported that he had the main responsibility, while the other noted that the mother had the main responsibility, which we might well have predicted.

Table 3.2 shows that those included in the main responsibility vary somewhat according to the family structures. In all of the lone mother families, and the vast majority of the mother and father households, the mother is one of those with the main responsibility for the decision about the secondary school. In rather less than two-thirds of the other types of family-household do we find that the mother is included in the main responsibility. In the traditional mother and father households the father was said to be included in the 'main' responsibility in about half of all families, compared with about one-fifth in lone mother families. On the other hand, in some two-parent households mothers have both the main and sole responsibility. For instance, in one two-parent family the father was interviewed but when asked about the main responsibility asserted that 'mother decides'.

In another family the mother who was interviewed said:

> I'm taking the main responsibility, he'll have the final choice. I've done all the leg work, I've done the viewing and sorting them all out but when it comes to the final crunch, he'll say, 'Right'. I expect [my daughter] will as well!

In yet another family the interviewed mother said: 'We both decided but I've done all the work'.

However, one mother asserted, in response to another question about the father's own educational experiences being relevant to his views on the child's education that:

> he said he would have liked her to go to [School A]. No he doesn't have an opinion — he's only the man in the house!

More interestingly, perhaps, the child is involved in the main responsibility in about a third of the mother and father families, compared with only about one in ten of the lone mother and other households. In other words, we have found that family structures do have an effect on the ways in which different family members are involved in the decisions about school 'choice' or 'placement'. However, given the complex analysis in terms of who had main responsibility and social background of the family, along with the relatively small sample size, it did not prove possible to distinguish the ways in which the main responsibility for secondary school choice related to social class.

The Other Parent's and the Child's Involvement in the Responsibility for the Choice Decision

The interviewee was asked whether the child's other parent (or significant other adults) was taking part in the decision about which school the child should go to. Eighty per cent of those interviewed said that the other parent was taking part and 20 per cent said that the other parent was not. In other words, the term 'main' is particularly significant in that the decision is a complex one involving usually two parents and generally the child, however varied the process might become.

Indeed, the child was involved in the process in the overwhelming number of families and, as we have noted in our discussion of Tables 3.1 and 3.2, they had or shared in the main responsibility in 22 per cent of families, even if they did not, on the whole, have the sole and main responsibility. In other words,

Table 3.3: Number of secondary schools child has talked to parents about

Number of schools	Percentage of parents (N = 70)
0	3
1	53
2	31
3	6
4 or more	7

children's involvement tended to be together with others, virtually never alone in making the final decision. The main responsibility was rarely left to the child. From the parents' point of view this may have been for entirely morally justifiable reasons — that they take the 'responsibility' for the child's education and upbringing seriously, as we mentioned in the introductory chapter. Indeed, it is interesting to note here that children are *not* entitled to fill in the transfer form nor expected to sign it. It is, however, in sharp contrast to the new conditions contained within the Children Act 1991, whereby children are given *greater rights* than hitherto. Yet, despite the Parent's Charter and the changing educational legislation children are not yet legally entitled formally to make this decision.

Indeed this follows what many of the parents felt was their *main* responsibility. For example, when some parents were asked the question about whether the child had talked about which school should be put on the form the following kinds of replies were made:

> Not really — he knows it isn't really up to him in the end. (Divorced mother)

> The final decision is the daughter's but the main responsibility is that of the grandmother, mother and child together. (Grandmother)

We noted above that a small minority of families felt that the child had had the main responsibility, although it is not very clear how the various different interviewees distinguished between the concept of 'main' and other sorts of responsibility. The concepts of 'main', 'sole' or 'final' responsibility require further investigation in relation to wider issues of education and upbringing.

In nearly all of the families (97 per cent) the child had talked about particular secondary schools with the person who was being interviewed. Table 3.3 gives the number of schools that the child and parent(s) had talked about. Over half of the children were reported to have talked about one secondary school with their parents and just under one-third were reported to have talked about two secondary schools. The fact that a little under half of the whole sample of target children had talked about more than one school bears testimony to their involvement in the process of decision-making.

However, it does not detract from the fact that, on the whole, they did not have the main responsibility for the decision, but rather exerted an influence over the process by discussing various options with their parents. It is likely that the parents used their roles and responsibilities as parents subtly and slowly — over perhaps a number of years — to influence the knowledge that children had available to them to take the main responsibility for choosing. It was in the minority of cases that the children were seen by the parents as having exerted the major influence over the decision. However, this could be seen as an ex-post rationalization and, indeed, it came from the parental interviews where it was unlikely that the majority of parents were going to admit to their ex-post rationalizations.

Conclusions

In this chapter we have begun the process of analysing how the different members of the family were involved in the process of making the decision about the secondary school to which the child would go. We have seen that, on the whole, most families interviewed felt that the *main* responsibility should rest with the parents whatever the family situation and/or gender or race of the child. In other words, we might surmise that parents regarded this decision as a particularly salient one for them as parents to take. However, we have yet to see whether it was felt to be a major decision or one that flowed from previous decisions within the family and at school. We shall begin to explore this matter in the next and subsequent chapters.

What is also clear from this brief analysis is that family structure or form is *not* the key criterion influencing how the decision is taken given that many lone parent families involve the albeit absent father and many two-parent families do not fully involve the present father. However, in the majority of families of whatever form or structure, the mother has, or shares, the main responsibility. This seems to flow almost automatically from her general responsibility for child care and child rearing. But this responsibility may be mediated by more or less liberal or authoritarian family patterns, in which decisions about schooling assume more awesome implications. This may mean that she has the *sole* responsibility, or that she has only the *initial* responsibility for doing the 'groundwork', or that she has the *final* responsibility. These issues may also be mediated by particular views of moral authority for children generally and in relation to education in particular. It is to these issues of the processes and content of the decision-making that we now turn.

Chapter 4

Parents' Appreciation of Procedures About School Transfer

Introduction

In this chapter we look at the choice process as a rational, purposive activity. We consider how the process of choosing schools began from the point of view of the target child's parents whom we interviewed, by discussing such issues as when they started thinking about secondary schooling, where they obtained information about schools, what information was particularly wanted and so on. In other words, we were particularly interested to look at factors related to the *procedures* involved in the transfer process and how the parents obtained sufficient information on which to make decisions about schools.

In subsequent chapters we shall explore the more substantive and social issues relating to school 'choice'. Here we are concerned to explore the extent to which the issue of choice was made salient to parents by different actions they undertook, and in addition, the extent to which parents used a range of resources and strategies to acquaint themselves with secondary schools in order to find out about the 'choice', or rather the options available from which to make a choice.

In looking at the ways in which families went about the process of choosing schools for their children when they were in their final year (Year 6) of primary school, before transferring to secondary school at the end of that academic session, we were also interested in establishing whether the procedures used by the schools and the LEAs were understood by the families involved in the transfer process. Moreover, we wanted to know whether the procedures amounted to what the families might consider to be choice processes or not. Finally, we were interested in whether or not changes in the policy context towards markets and consumerism had taken effect and thereby influenced these parents and whether or not they felt themselves to have become consumers. The parents we interviewed were asked a series of questions about the process of choosing secondary schools — ranging from when they began to think about it to how they reached the ultimate decision, including what kinds of information they sought.

Table 4.1: *When secondary schooling was first considered by parents*

First considered secondary schooling	Percentage of parents* [N = 70]
Fourth Year Junior (Year 6)	44
Third Year Junior (Year 5)	33
Second Year Junior (Year 4)	14
First Year Junior (Year 3)	4
Infant school	4

Note: * Percentages do not add up to 100 because of rounding.

Initial Thoughts on Secondary Schools

We were concerned to find out when the whole process of considering secondary schooling started and so we began by asking the parents *when* they started thinking seriously about secondary schools for their child and whether it was before they were prompted to do so by the various education authorities or schools that were involved. The parents' responses are shown in Table 4.1.

We found that over two-fifths of the parents started thinking seriously about secondary schools for their child during the child's final year of junior schooling (Year 6), but that a significant proportion — one-third — had started thinking about this issue in the third year (Year 5). Nearly a quarter of parents had started thinking about secondary schools even earlier than that. So there were interesting variations between the parents in terms of when they first began to think about schools or rather their initial thoughts on secondary schools; we shall return to discuss this issue of the social process later. Here, we start by analysing the parents' replies to this kind of question as the beginnings of the rather formal school procedures.

There were no significant differences between the parents of girls and boys on this question of initial thoughts, or between parents in the two boroughs. However, there were some differences between other groups of parents. Interestingly, nearly all the parents of the black and Asian target children started thinking seriously about secondary schooling in Year 6 and as a corollary, it was largely the parents of white children who started thinking about this issue prior to this time.

In terms of family structure there were also differences (although it should be noted that these did not reach statistical significance). Over half (56 per cent) of lone mother families (of which there were sixteen) only started to think about secondary schools in Year 6, compared with just under two-fifths (39 per cent) of mother and father families (of which there were forty-one) and half in mother and partner families (of which there were four). In other words, we may speculate that lone parent families may start thinking about secondary schools *later* than two-parent households, and that this may have something to do with the burdens of being a lone parent family. However, as we saw in Chapter 3, many of the lone mother families involved the child's father in

Table 4.2:   Parents considering different numbers of secondary schools

Number of schools	Percentage of parents (N = 70)
One	23
Two	36
Three	11
Four	20
Five	6
Six	1
Seven	3

the decision-making process where he was available. On the other hand, many mothers in two-parent households began the process early and alone in terms of what they called 'doing the groundwork', as we also noted above in Chapter 3.

We also found an interesting and statistically significant difference between families in terms of the father's socio-economic background and when parents first started thinking about secondary schools. Significantly more families where the father was from a non-manual than a manual social background (48 per cent compared with 23 per cent) started thinking about secondary schooling when their child was in Year 5, that is, the penultimate year rather than the final year of primary school. Overall, we found that two-thirds of families with fathers from non-manual backgrounds started thinking about a secondary school *before* the last year of primary school, whereas for those in other families almost half had not started thinking about this issue until Year 6 of primary school. In other words, it could be argued that the social class of the father was very important in determining how much forethought was given to types of secondary school.

Our next concern was to try and establish how many secondary schools parents initially thought about for their child. They were therefore asked to name those secondary schools they had been thinking about for their child as a prelude to talking about the salient features of those schools in terms of reasons for the choice. The *numbers* of schools that were being considered by parents are shown in Table 4.2.

The majority of parents named more than one school that they had been thinking about, making it clear that the parents whom we interviewed felt that they did have some options available. However, nearly a quarter of the parents were thinking about just *one* school. Around one-third were considering two schools (36 per cent) or three to four schools (31 per cent) and one in ten were considering between five and seven schools. This means, in effect, that three-quarters of the parents in our study had at least given some consideration to alternative schools and some of these we can surmise were 'very active' choosers. However, the question of whether thinking about more than one school constitutes a 'choice' is something to which we will give greater consideration below.

Transfer Procedure, 'Choice' and Understanding

We wanted to find out how well parents understood the actual formal transfer process. If parents are to be able to use their power as 'consumers' effectively, they need to know *how* the administrative system itself works. We were particularly interested to find out about parents' awareness about the whole procedure for transferring from primary to secondary school.

First of all, we asked them what they understood about the procedure for transferring schools and, on the basis of their answers to this question, the interviewers made a subjective rating of the respondents' understanding of the transfer procedure. We found that over half of those interviewed (53 per cent) seemed to understand the procedure well; over one-third (36 per cent) did not seem to understand, while 11 per cent thought that they did understand, but in fact they did not appear to have grasped the relevant procedures.

We also asked parents some more specific questions about the procedure. In particular, we wanted to know whether they were aware of the criteria used by schools for admitting pupils. We found that over half of the parents (56 per cent) felt that they understood all the criteria, while over one-fifth (23 per cent) understood some of the criteria. However, nearly one-fifth (16 per cent) did *not* understand the admissions criteria and 6 per cent did not know. This means that well over a fifth of the parents were not aware of how the schools they were applying to for their child actually made decisions about which pupils would be admitted. It is thus clear that a significant minority of parents are not clear about the transfer process or the admissions criteria used by schools.

We also asked a question about the appeals procedure that parents can institute if they do not get offered a place at their preferred secondary school. We were keen to establish whether parents knew first of all that they *could* appeal, and second, whether they knew *how* to appeal. We found that two-fifths of the parents who answered this question (N = 60) knew how to appeal, while one-third knew that they could appeal, but did not know how to go about it; around a quarter of the parents (27 per cent) did not know about the procedure. In other words, a large minority of parents were not clear about the precise details of the appeals procedure — either to the local education authority, or directly to the school — if their child was not allocated their preferred school.

We can see, therefore, that a significant proportion of parents do not appear to have the necessary information or knowledge to be able effectively to exercise their power in relation to choosing schools. They do not know how schools or LEAs decide which pupils to admit, or how they go about an appeal if they do not get their preferred choice. The whole transfer process for some parents can be a very worrisome or stressful one and we wanted to try and establish whether our sample of parents experienced such stress. The interviewers thus made a subjective rating as to the 'parents' anxiety', as they perceived it, about the whole process of 'choosing secondary schools', giving us some indication of how worrisome or stressful the process might be. Our

Table 4.3: How useful parents found the interview with the headteacher

Usefulness of interview	Percentage of parents (N = 64)*
Helpful	58
Formality	16
Not very helpful	19
Concern about school chosen	8

*Note: * N is less than 70 as six parents had not had an interview with the headteacher. And percentages do not add to 100 because of rounding.*

findings indicated that some parents found the procedure more stressful than others. Over a quarter (26 per cent) of the interviewees were perceived by the interviewers to be 'extremely' anxious, just under a third (30 per cent) to be 'somewhat' anxious, while just over a third (36 per cent) were not perceived to be anxious. In 9 per cent of the families it was not possible to say whether parents were anxious or not. In other words, we surmise that the process of 'choosing a secondary school' is indeed seen as stressful by the majority of parents in this study, even if they are not fully aware of what there is to choose from — or rather, what schools their children are likely to be admitted to.

In both Camden and Wandsworth, the actual transfer procedure involved the parents being invited to an interview with the headteacher of their child's primary school to discuss which schools the parents would be applying to for their child. We therefore asked them whether they had had such an interview/ discussion with their child's primary school headteacher about the transfer to secondary school. Almost all of the parents (91 per cent) reported that they had had such a discussion. The six parents who had not been to speak to the headteacher gave a variety of reasons as to why they had not had this meeting — for example, they had no need because they knew the procedures or they were not offered the interview.

We wanted to find out whether this meeting was considered to have been useful, and so we asked an open-ended question, categorizing the responses *post hoc*. Table 4.3 reports the results that emerged. Over half of the parents found the interview with the headteacher useful, while 16 per cent felt that the interview was merely a formality as they had other children and had been through the transfer process before. Nearly one-fifth of the parents did not find the interview very helpful, often because they felt that they knew what they had to do, and just under one in ten mentioned that the headteacher was concerned about their choice.

These views on the helpfulness of the interview with the headteacher varied according to the family structure. The vast majority of lone-mother families found the interview very helpful (81 per cent), whereas only just over half of the mother and father families did, and only just over a third of mother and partner families did. Of course, we should note here the very small numbers

Table 4.4: How parents found out about preferred school

How parents found out about preferred school	Without prompting Percentage of parents (N = 70)	With and without prompting Percentage of parents (N = 70)
Visits	41 (1)	63 (1)
Friends/neighbours	34 (2)	59 (2)
School brochure	31 (3)	49 (3)
Other parents	26	40
Other children in family	24	27
Local school	21	24
Primary headteacher	11	14

in each group. Nevertheless, it is very interesting to note that thirteen of the sixteen lone mother families found the interview helpful and this may connect with the fact that they had only just begun the formal process of consideration, unlike the other kinds of families.

The majority of black and Asian parents found the interview helpful, whereas only about half of the white families did. This may be because more of the white families were familiar with the procedures. There was no difference between the parents' views on the usefulness of the headteacher's interview in terms of the sex of the child. However, one interesting finding relates to differences between families of different social classes, but only when using the father's social class. Only a minority of families with fathers from professional/managerial occupational backgrounds (30 per cent) found the interview with the headteacher useful, while the vast majority of families with fathers from skilled (59 per cent) and semi-skilled (100 per cent) occupational backgrounds did so. We have already mentioned that the former group of families tended to be those who had thought about the processes in the years before the final year of primary school and they may therefore have done the necessary ground work not to have to rely on the interview with the headteacher.

How Parents Found Out About Schools

We were very interested to find out how parents found out about the various different schools and the types of information they sought out and used in helping them to come to a decision about which particular schools they should apply to for their child. First of all, they were asked how they had found out about the school that they had named as their preferred school. Table 4.4 gives those reasons spontaneously mentioned by 10 per cent or more of parents and the same reasons mentioned after prompting.

The three answers given most frequently, both spontaneously and after prompting in relation to finding out about the preferred secondary school, were visits (41 per cent and 63 per cent), friends or neighbours (34 and 59 per cent) and the school's information booklet (31 and 49 per cent). In relation to the answers that emerged spontaneously, visits were also the most frequently mentioned means of finding out whatever the type of the family structure. Friends and neighbours figured slightly more prominently for lone mother families (44 per cent) than for mother and father (32 per cent) and mother and partner (38 per cent) families, although again the small numbers in each of these categories should be borne in mind.

In about a quarter of all families there was another child in the family that affected the choice of preferred school and similarly other parents influenced the decision for just over a quarter of families, especially lone mother and mother and father families. The fact that the school was local was more important to mother and father families than it was to lone mother families.

There were some differences between families on the basis of the child's sex, ethnicity and the family's social class background. Visits were mentioned slightly more often by the parents of boys than girls (50 versus 32 per cent) as were booklets (44 versus 18 per cent). Neither visits, friends/neighbours nor other parents distinguished between families from different ethnic groups but the local school was somewhat more important for white than black or Asian families, albeit that extremely small numbers are involved in the latter groups.

There were also some distinctions to be drawn in terms of social class. Both visits and booklets were noticeably (although not statistically significantly) more important for families where the mother's social class background was professional/managerial or non-manual (office) or the father's was professional/managerial than for those from other social class backgrounds. On the other hand, a local school and other children in the family seemed to figure more for families where the father's occupational background was skilled manual or those where the mother's social class background was semi-skilled or unskilled.

In relation to the answers about sources of information that emerged with and without prompting, there were some more interesting differences — although not statistically significant — reported in these sources of information between the two boroughs. In particular, more parents in Camden than in Wandsworth reported that they knew about the school because it was local, or through friends and neighbours, or other parents, whereas more parents in Wandsworth knew about the school through visits, or the primary school head. There are clearly procedural and possibly other differences, such as cultural or social networks between the two boroughs, in how familiar parents become with the various schools.

Links with Schools and Information about Schools

A series of questions was asked about the links that existed with secondary schools and information about secondary schools. Parents were asked questions

Table 4.5:   Percentage of parents reporting various links

Links	Percentage of parents (N = 70)
Child's friends plan to go to school	83
Child's friends go to school	63
Someone parent knows goes there	51
Someone parent knows works at school	29
Siblings at school	23
Other relatives are pupils at school	16
Child's parent (or significant adult) went to school	14
Other (child) relatives plan to go to school	7
Siblings went to school	4

Table 4.6:   Types of brochures read

Type of brochure	Percentage of parents (N = 66)
Individual schools in borough	76
Borough booklet	56
LEA schools outside borough	39
Grant-maintained schools	24
City technology college	23
Private schools	21

similar to those noted above, about how they knew about their named/preferred school and whether any family members or friends went to, or were planning to go to, the school they preferred/wanted (or would most like) their child to go to. Table 4.5 gives the percentage of parents reporting various links.

Over eight out of ten parents (83 per cent) reported that some of their child's friends *planned* to go to the same school as they wanted their own child to go to. Nearly two-thirds of the parents (63 per cent) said that friends of their child *currently went* to the school, and about half of the parents (51 per cent) knew someone who went there. One of the main factors cited above for knowledge of the preferred school was either school brochures or visits to the school. Altogether, 94 per cent of the parents had read at least one brochure about secondary schools. Although 6 per cent of the parents had not read any brochures, around a third (31 per cent) had read either one or two brochures, or three or four brochures (33 per cent) or between five and nine brochures (30 per cent).

We asked parents which brochures they had read. Table 4.6 gives the percentage of parents who had read different types of brochures. Over three-quarters (76 per cent) of the parents had read brochures about individual schools within their own borough and just over half (56 per cent) had read the booklet produced by the borough. Over a third (39 per cent) of the parents had read brochures about LEA (county or voluntary) schools outside the

Table 4.7: Usefulness of examination results section

Usefulness of exam results section	Percentage of parents (N = 70)
Did not see brochures/exam section	31
Very useful	17
Quite useful	29
Not very useful	10
Not at all useful	7
No section	6

Table 4.8: Comments on utility of examination results section

Kinds of use of exam results section	Percentage of parents (N = 41)
Add to overall picture	29
Confusing/difficult to understand	27
Useful comparison	22
Particularly wanted to see	10
Standard format needed	10
Selective/misleading	7

Note: Percentages add up to more than 100 as more than one reason was sometimes given.

borough. Around a quarter of those interviewed had read brochures about grant-maintained schools (24 per cent), the city technology college in Wandsworth (23 per cent) or private schools (21 per cent).

The vast majority of parents (91 per cent) who had read brochures found them useful. A quarter of these parents (N = 60) felt that brochures 'tell you what is going on in school' but a similar number (23 per cent) felt that they were of limited use. Ten per cent of parents felt that brochures helped them compare schools. However, the same percentage felt that brochures only 'tell you what they want to tell' or that the schools needed to be visited as well.

Parents were asked how useful they found the section in the brochures on examination results. Table 4.7 gives their responses. Around a third of the parents had not seen the examination results section. However, nearly one-fifth (17 per cent) found this section of the brochure 'very useful'. Over a quarter (29 per cent) found it 'quite useful'. Nearly one-fifth (17 per cent) did not think the section was useful, and 6 per cent reported that there was no section on examination results in their brochure.

We also asked parents in what ways they found the examination results useful (or not) and we had replies from 59 per cent of the parents. The parents' responses were categorized and Table 4.8 gives the percentage of parents making comments relating to specific issues. Over a quarter of the parents felt that the examination results section 'added to the overall picture' (29 per cent), but a similar proportion found the section confusing or difficult to understand (27 per cent). Just over a fifth felt that the section provided a useful comparison. Some of the comments that the parents made included:

It's not always the most important thing, exam results. It's useful as a guide.

It was very useful as a comparison between the schools to see what expectations they had of their pupils.

That was very useful . . . I'm sure they could be presented in a more parent-friendly way.

Some schools are better at one subject than another, so it's not easy to make a comparison.

I found it very difficult to understand . . . they were quite useful but I think . . . they write them in such a way that each school will look good anyway.

It wasn't very useful . . . they're confusing, all these grids and things. They could just put them out straightforward.

Didn't really understand it. The only sort of thing I understand is ten out of ten or stuff like that.

I get very confused with all the figures and everything.

They're all totally meaningless.

Although almost three-quarters of the parents had seen the examination results of the school(s) they were interested in, they had not necessarily seen them in the school brochure. Other sources of information in addition to brochures were local newspapers (mentioned by 13 per cent), secondary school staff (7 per cent), other parents (7 per cent), friends/people at work (6 per cent) and primary school staff (1 per cent). Although the brochure was the main source of information, we can see from these findings that parents sought out examination results from a variety of sources.

Moreover, examination results are not necessarily either seen as salient features of a school advertising itself for future generations of children despite the policy regulations or rhetoric, nor do parents necessarily see examination results as the *key* issue in deciding upon a school. This seems to be quite at odds with the current policy debate about school league tables on examination results to which we referred in the introduction. However, we shall return to this issue again below, as a substantive rather than procedural one, in Chapters 5 and 6.

Table 4.9: Sources of information mentioned

Source of information	Without prompting Percentage of parents (N = 70)	With and without prompting Percentage of parents (N = 68)
Friends	34 (1)	60 (2)
Parents of children at secondary school	33 (2)	51
Children, including siblings	31 (3)	63 (1)
Parents of children at preferred secondary school	30	54 (3)
Primary school teachers/ headteacher	29	43
Parents of children at primary school	26	54 (3)
Relatives	19	32
Neighbours	14	28
Articles in the press	13	32
Adults working in education	10	22
Work colleagues	9	26
Advertisements	6	21

We also tried to consider other sources of information about schools. Parents were asked how they had found out about schools for their child apart from reading brochures. This was followed with questions about what they had wanted to find out and whether they had succeeded in this objective. Table 4.9 gives the specific sources of information mentioned without prompting by 6 per cent or more of the sample. It also gives the percentage who reported having obtained information from these sources with and without prompting.

Four sources of information were each spontaneously mentioned by around a third of the parents, namely: friends (34 per cent); parents of children at secondary school (33 per cent); children, including siblings (31 per cent); and parents with children at their *preferred* secondary school (30 per cent). Over a quarter of the parents mentioned getting information from primary school teachers or headteachers (29 per cent) or parents of children at primary school (26 per cent). Three of the four sources of information that were mentioned most frequently spontaneously were also reported most frequently after prompting. However, the order varied, with children, including siblings being mentioned by nearly two-thirds (63 per cent), friends by slightly fewer (60 per cent), parents of children at their preferred secondary school by just over half (54 per cent) and parents of children at *primary* school being mentioned with the same frequency (54 per cent).

These sources of information are notable in that friends are again a powerful source of information; other parents, other children, including siblings and primary school teachers/headteachers are all very important for large sections of the sample. However, this list also includes some additional factors, such as articles in the media and advertisements, as well as parents' work colleagues. We might surmise that the fact that advertisements featured is a function of the

Table 4.10: When parents obtained information

When the child was in . . .	Percentage of parents (N = 70)
Fourth Year Juniors (Year 6)	73
Third Year Juniors (Year 5)	36
Second Year Juniors (Year 4)	23
First Year Juniors (Year 3)	6
Infant school	4

changing climate under open enrollment, with schools trying to maximize the number of applicants and hence new entrants (and associated funding) to the school.

Parents were asked *when* they obtained information about the schools or talked to people about them. Table 4.10 gives their responses. We found that nearly three-quarters of the parents (73 per cent) obtained information while their child was in the last year of primary school (Year 6); a significant proportion (36 per cent) obtained information while their child was in Year 5 and over a fifth (23 per cent) while she or he was in Year 4. This means that only a minority of parents in the sample had actively sought out information about schools before the target child's final year of primary school. This finding chimes with that earlier in this chapter that most parents start thinking about specific schools in their child's last year. However, it may be the case that at least some of the mothers who laid the ground for the 'choice' may be those who had obtained information earlier than Year 6.

Types of Information Wanted, such as Examination Results

We also asked the parents a series of questions to establish the sorts of things they wanted to know about secondary schools. First, they were asked what sort of information they were looking for about secondary schools. Table 4.11 gives details of the types of information spontaneously mentioned by 10 per cent or more of the sample and those mentioned after prompting with the first four types of information only.

Half of the parents spontaneously mentioned wanting information about the academic side of the school or subjects offered. One-third were looking for A level examination results and a similar number for GCSE results or the general atmosphere/feel of the school. Our findings suggest that information about academic subjects is more important for middle-class families, while exam results are mentioned most frequently by working-class families. It is possible, however, that these findings could be the result of middle-class families being more explicit about the sorts of information they were looking for.

These small social class differences are also reflected in the approaches of the different family types. Over half of mother and father families (56 per cent)

Table 4.11: Types of information parents were looking for

Types of information	Without prompting Percentage of parents (N = 70)	With and without prompting Percentage of parents (N = 70)
Academic side/subjects offered	50	87
A level results	33	60
GCSE results	30	60
General atmosphere/feel	30	51
Specific subjects	24	—
Discipline/behaviour/bullying	21	—
Teachers/teacher–pupil relations	14	—
Type of children at school	13	—
Class size	11	—
Facilities	10	—

had looked for academic subjects, whereas only 44 per cent of lone mother families had. Over a third of mother and father families (37 per cent) mentioned looking for GCSE results without prompting, whereas only 19 per cent of lone mother families did. Similarly, almost half (42 per cent) of mother and father families looked for A levels, whereas only 19 per cent of lone mother families did.

We also prompted parents about whether specific types of information had been sought — namely details of the academic side of the school, its general atmosphere and examination results — if they had not been mentioned spontaneously. Nearly nine out of ten parents, after prompting, mentioned that they were looking for information about the academic side of the school or subjects offered. Nearly two-thirds wanted details of the school's examination results and around half wanted to know about the school's general atmosphere/feel.

These types of information were not different for boys or girls or for children from different ethnic groups whether spontaneously mentioned or after prompting. When the spontaneous and prompted answers were added together there were no differences between the parents in Camden and Wandsworth, although there were some differences in terms of just the spontaneous answers around looking for academic subjects (39 per cent in Camden and 62 per cent in Wandsworth), looking at A levels (28 per cent in Camden; 38 per cent in Wandsworth) and looking for feel/atmosphere (in Camden only 42 per cent felt it important whereas in Wandsworth 65 per cent did so).

It is interesting to note that although parents were looking for factors such as academic subjects, atmosphere or A level or GCSE examination results, they did not necessarily find the information about examination results that easy to understand or that useful, once they had obtained it. We propose to examine this issue in future research as we feel that the contradictory findings merit further investigation.

Finally, parents were asked whether their child had had any extra educational help outside school (e.g. private tutoring, attending a Saturday

Table 4.12: Number of secondary schools visited

Number of schools visited	Percentage of parents (N = 70)
None	13
One	21
Two	23
Three	20
Four to eight	23

Table 4.13: Percentage of parents applying to different numbers of secondary schools

Number of schools applied to	Percentage of parents (N = 70)
One	53
Two	27
Three	6
Four	10
Five	4

school) within the last two years. Over eight out of ten parents (83 per cent) reported that she or he had not had any such help, while 10 per cent said that they had. A further 7 per cent said that they had had extra help for entrance examinations to private schools.

Visits to Secondary Schools

Given that almost half of the parents (over 40 per cent) had mentioned that they knew about their preferred school through visits to secondary schools, we also asked a series of questions about visits to potential secondary schools. First, parents were asked how many secondary schools they had visited (with a view to their child going there). Table 4.12 gives their responses.

Perhaps the most interesting finding is that over one in ten parents (13 per cent) had *not* visited *any* secondary schools, whilst around one-fifth had visited one school (21 per cent), two schools (23 per cent), three schools (20 per cent) or four or more schools (23 per cent). However, half of those who had not visited any secondary schools (four out of nine), intended to visit one school for their child's interview for a place at that school.

Chosen Schools on the Transfer Form

All of the parents reported in the interviews that they had already made the decision about which secondary schools would be put down on the transfer forms or which school they would apply to. Table 4.13 gives the percentage of parents applying to different numbers of secondary schools.

Table 4.14: *Do you see yourself as a 'consumer of education'?*

Are you a consumer of education?	Percentage of parents (N = 70)*
Yes (spontaneous)	21
Yes (after explanation)	7
No (spontaneous)	14
No (after explanation)	49
Don't know	7
Parents differ	1

Note: * Percentages do not add up to 100 because of rounding.

Around half of the parents reported that they had, in the event, only applied to one school (53 per cent); over a quarter (27 per cent) had applied to two schools; 6 per cent had applied to three and 10 per cent had applied to four schools; 4 per cent had applied to five schools. In other words, at the end of the 'decision-making process', about half the parents in this sample felt that they had more than one school to which they could apply, even if, as we shall see below, some parents did not necessarily see this as a 'real choice', but rather as a compromise. The remainder, however, had decided that it would suffice to apply to one school only.

We also asked whether the child had talked about which schools should be put down on the transfer form or which school he or she should go to. We found that virtually *all* the parents (99 per cent) said that she or he had. As we noted in Chapter 3, although parents, and especially mothers, felt they had the main responsibility, children were usually involved and/or consulted and, in some cases, made or helped to make the 'final' decision. Given this, it is a pity that children cannot make their own preferences clear by having at least to put their signature on the form together with that of their parents'.

Finally, parents were asked whether they saw themselves as 'consumers of education'. We were keen to establish whether or not the national policy rhetoric had percolated down to the school level. Over half the parents (56 per cent) did not understand what was meant by the question and an explanation had to be provided. Table 4.14 gives the responses for the whole sample of parents.

Altogether, nearly two-thirds of the parents did *not* see themselves as consumers of education, while just over a quarter (28 per cent) did. Certainly this does not seem to indicate that many parents had taken on board the policy rhetoric. But we will now look at whether or not parents consider a range of substantive factors in relation to secondary school 'choice' to flesh out whether or not parents' actions may be construed as implying that they are, in fact, 'consumers of education'.

Conclusions

In this chapter we have reviewed the processes gone through and the procedures involved in making a decision about secondary school by looking at how the parents felt about the formal transfer process, the information that they gathered on which to make a decision and how they themselves went about the process in terms of soliciting information from friends, relatives, neighbours and so on, as well as teachers, headteachers and visits to schools. We also looked at what they felt about the quality of information on offer such as the headteachers' interviews and the school brochures/prospectuses, and, in particular, the information on examination results. We have also compared their spontaneous responses on what they were looking for in terms of information on secondary schools.

We have been able to consider the choice process as both a cognitive and social process. We considered parents' views on brochures and published exam results (Tables 4.6–4.8). We also found social contacts to be a key feature. Friends and neighbours, other parents and other children are all vitally important (Tables 4.4 and 4.9) in affecting parents' views of secondary schools. The presence of existing links with particular schools was also significant (Table 4.5). Finally, parents also clearly value what they can see with their own eyes (Table 4.4) — 'We liked what we saw'. This includes both specific visits to schools on their open evenings, and also observations made about schools in the vicinity, for example, in terms of the behaviour of pupils as they go to and from school. In all this it is clear that parents are offered certain alternatives and seek out for themselves certain information about different schools. However, it is not clear whether they feel, at the end of the day, that they have, in fact, been offered realistic alternatives, nor may they wish to have them if they already hold sufficient information within the family or household on which to base their 'choice'. This is an issue to which we will return later. However, we turn now to what parents considered the most important factors in the 'choice' of secondary school, before moving on to consider whether there are any factors that would detract from families choosing certain schools.

Chapter 5

Parents' Reasons for Choice of Preferred Secondary School

Introduction

This chapter is about the kinds of reasons parents offered, in response to a variety of questions, about their choices of, or preferences for, particular schools. In other words, we begin to look at the substantive content of the decision processes, having looked at the kinds of processes and procedures that parents had gone through to reach these decisions. In this chapter we are particularly interested in the *positive* reasons for the choice of school, both in terms of the general issues and also in terms of the particular schools preferred. In the next chapter we shall look at the *negative* evaluations of schools, or rather the reasons why parents did not choose, or even rejected, certain schools.

We start by looking at the reasons parents offered for their serious consideration of named schools. Then we move on to a more general discussion of the preferred schools and from there into an even more general discussion of factors relating to choice of school. We asked a series of questions to tap parents' thinking about what they were looking for. As these questions progressed to some extent we pinned parents down to specify their three main reasons in order of priority.

Different responses and different emphases emerged in the answers given to these various ways of asking these questions. To some extent, people may have been elaborating and going into more detail as the questions progressed, but on the other hand, at times they appeared to be trying to be helpful, and to be searching to find something new to say. Some questions were also quite open-ended while others included prompts, and there are apparent differences between prompted and unprompted answers. It may also be the case that some questions tap more into the choice process as one of the social interactions occurring in particular concrete contexts, while other questions tap more into the choice process as one of a cognitive and rational weighing up of information and parental values. The initial open-ended questions incline more towards the former, while the concluding question, asking parents to list their three most important reasons, inclines more towards the latter.

Table 5.1: Percentage of different types of schools named

Type of school named	Percentage of responses (N = 189)*
LEA Mixed (C/V)	25
LEA Girls (C/V)	14
LEA Boys (C/V)	10
Out of LEA (C/V)	22
Grant-maintained	10
City Technology College	8
Private	11

Note: * This refers to the total number of responses made.

As a result, different sorts of answers emerge. Proximity to the home thus appears much more significant in some answers than others (e.g. contrast Tables 5.2, 5.5 and 5.8), while the presence of existing links with schools appears significant at some times and not at others. Rather than regarding these shifts in responses as problematic, or regarding some of these answers as more 'valid' than others, we suggest that they are all valid indicators of the varied and complex processes that are involved in the eventual 'choice' or 'placement' of particular children in particular schools.

Types of Schools Named and/or Preferred

As we mentioned in the previous chapter we asked parents to tell us about the schools they were considering for their children in the process of reaching a decision about which schools to apply for. Some parents only named *one* school that they were considering, but the majority were able to name more than one and sometimes up to six or seven (see Table 4.2 for details). We have analysed the first three schools named by the parents as state or independent schools.

The *type* of school named varied. However, state schools (either LEA or grant-maintained) were named in the vast majority of cases and these were generally in the same borough as the primary school, as opposed to outside the borough. Private schools were named least frequently — only one in ten parents named a private school as their first named school, and in the case of the other named schools, fewer parents still named such a school. In other words, the vast majority of parents considered only state secondary schools, for the most part within the borough, with only a very small minority of families considering a private school for their child. We also looked in more detail at the different types of schools named, and in particular at the range of schools that were being considered. The percentages of different types of schools named are shown in Table 5.1.

One quarter of all the state schools named were LEA financed mixed county or voluntary (C/V) schools within the borough. A similar proportion

Table 5.2: *Reasons why parents had been thinking about named secondary schools: First, second and third named schools*

Reason for thinking about named school	First named school Percentage of parents (N = 70)	Second named school Percentage of parents (N = 53)	Third named school Percentage of parents (N = 28)
Near to home	19 (1)	13 (2)	14 (3)
Siblings went there	19 (2)	—	11
Good reputation	17 (3)	17 (1)	—
Like what they saw/ know school	16	11	—
Know children	16	—	—
Good academic results	14	11	18 (2)
Child wants to go	13	—	—
Single-sex	10	—	—
Recommended	10	—	—
Facilities	—	13 (2)	—
Local school	—	—	21 (1)
Parent/relative link	—	—	11
Church school	—	—	11

were LEA-financed single-sex schools in the borough. Just over one-fifth of the schools named were LEA-financed county or voluntary schools in another borough. Ten per cent of the schools named were grant-maintained. Eight per cent of the responses were to the city technology college in Wandsworth and just over one in ten were to private schools. Although the new types of schools were only named on relatively few occasions, it is important to note that there is only *one* CTC in one of the two boroughs. In addition, there were no grant-maintained schools in Camden (although there were some in neighbouring boroughs) and only one in Wandsworth at the time our study began. The fact that nearly a fifth of the responses related to these schools is therefore worth noting.

Reasons for Thinking about Named Schools

We then asked parents *why* they had been thinking about these schools that they had named. We were interested in exploring the kinds of reasons offered for all the schools that the parents were considering, even though not all parents were considering more than one. We wanted to look at the reasons for the consideration of preferred schools. We also wanted to consider the reasons for *not* choosing a school, which we will look at in the next chapter.

Here we will start by analysing the reasons offered for the preferred schools, by looking separately at up to three named schools. We looked at the reasons offered for the first, second and third named schools. A very wide range of responses emerged. These were categorized and those reasons mentioned by 10 per cent or more of the parents for the first three named schools are shown in Table 5.2.

Table 5.3: *Reason why parents were thinking about secondary schools*

Composite reason for thinking about named school	Percentage of parents (N = 70)
Good reputation	44
Near to home	37
Good academic results	36
Liked what they saw/know school	33
Siblings there/went there	29
Recommended	29
Know children there/friends	27
Single-sex	27
Local school	24
Church school (RC/CE)	20
Facilities/opportunities	20
Child wants to go there	19
Good education	17
Teachers/headteacher	16
Suits child	16
New/exciting/technology/well-funded	14
Small school	13
Subjects offered	13
Mixed school	13
Parent/relative link	11
Cater for special needs	11
Easy to get to	10
Discipline/behaviour	10
Atmosphere/ethos	10
No other choice	10

As we can see, parents gave rather different reasons for thinking about each of the first three schools that they named. For the *first-named school,* the school being *near to home* and siblings at the school were the reasons most frequently mentioned, followed by the school's reputation. For the *second-named school,* the school's *reputation* was most frequently mentioned followed by proximity to home and the school's facilities. For the *third-named school,* the fact that it was *local* emerged most frequently, followed by its academic record. What is also interesting, is that good academic results and proximity to home were the only two reasons to be mentioned by more than 10 per cent of the parents for each of these three schools. The most important difference to note at this stage between specific groups of parents was that a *single-sex* school was cited as a reason more often by parents of *girls* than boys, a point to which we shall return later in this chapter. Somewhat more parents of boys than girls cited a school's good reputation and the fact that it was near to home or a local school.

We then put the reasons together into a composite group to try to identify the key reasons given as a form of summary. When all the reasons given were combined together a different picture emerged as shown in Table 5.3.

The reason that most frequently occurred was the school's *reputation* (mentioned by nearly half of the parents), followed by its *proximity* to home and its academic results or *performance*. However, these three main reasons are not the same for both boys and girls. A good reputation was mentioned more often for boys than girls (twenty-two responses versus nine). On the other hand, single-sex schooling is mentioned very frequently for girls but not for boys (eighteen responses versus one).

In addition to getting parents to list their reasons for considering particular secondary schools, they were also asked to make general comments. Some of the comments they made included:

> A single-sex school because she gets easily distracted and the academic record. My sister went there and her father's sisters all went there and it's got a good track record. It has very high standards . . . and it's like an independent school.

> We always thought of [School Y]. We know it was an ex-grammar school and had a good reputation. But always around here I thought it was a good school for a boy.

> She took the decision out of our hands completely because she had decided where she wanted to go and she wasn't interested in looking anywhere else at all.

> The position of the school . . . in this day and age I wouldn't want a boy of his age to be travelling in certain areas, certain distances . . . I think it's dangerous.

Views About the Preferred/Chosen School

Narrowing the focus down, parents were also asked a series of questions about the school they had actually applied to or, in the case of those who were applying to more than one school, their preferred school. In Table 5.1, we presented the *type* of schools named, in terms of both their 'financial' or 'governmental' status and whether or not they were coeducational. We also addressed the issue of whether or not parents were seriously considering independent as opposed to state schools. In Table 5.4, we look at just their first named or preferred school, rather than a composite of all named schools. *Around a quarter of the parents* stated that they had applied to or preferred an *LEA mixed school*, and just over a fifth preferred an *LEA girls' school*. A boys' school was named by 14 per cent and a school in another LEA by just under a fifth of parents. Small numbers of parents named a grant-maintained school, a city technology college (all Wandsworth parents) or a private school.

We asked parents an open-ended question about *what they liked* about their preferred school. Their responses were categorized and Table 5.5 gives those reasons mentioned by 10 per cent or more of the parents. Over two-fifths

Table 5.4:   Secondary school preferred by parents

Type of school preferred	Percentage of parents (N = 66)
LEA Mixed (C/V)	26
LEA Girls (C/V)	21
LEA Boys (C/V)	14
Out of LEA (C/V)	17
City technology college	9
Grant-maintained	7
Private	6

Table 5.5:   Reasons parents liked their preferred school

Reason liked named school	Percentage of parents (N = 70)
Subjects/facilities	41
Atmosphere/ethos	27
Academic results	27
First impressions	23
Environment/building	21
Discipline	21
Single-sex	16
Staff/headteacher	14
Small school	13
Near to home	11
Way teaching organized	10

of the parents liked the subjects/facilities at their preferred school, over a quarter mentioned the atmosphere/ethos or academic results and over one-fifth were impressed when they visited the school (23 per cent), liked the environment/buildings (21 per cent) or discipline in the school (21 per cent). Given the ambiguity of meaning about the term 'discipline' in this context and the fact that more than one in five parents used it as a reason for the preferred school we shall have occasion to return to this subject in Chapter 6. Parents made a variety of comments about why they liked certain schools, for example:

We were impressed with the subjects that were on offer.

We were impressed with the sort of intangible, with the atmosphere of the school. You actually walked in there and you felt the sense of calm.

These reasons for liking the preferred school were not the same for the parents of boys as for girls. In fact, two very important and statistically significant differences emerged, namely that more parents of *girls* than boys liked the schools that they were applying to because they were *small* (24 versus 3 per cent) and that they were *single-sex* (27 versus 3 per cent). One mother gave the following reason:

Can't really say. I mean, it's close to us. Me and my husband liked it because there's no big main roads for her to cross, which is good. [Kim] is very quiet and that [would have] worried us if she went to . . . a mixed school.

Similarly, the reasons for liking the preferred schools varied between families with children from different ethnic groups. Compared with white families, black, Asian and other families made reference to 'discipline' more often (35 versus 16 per cent). Moreover black parents plumped for 'first impressions' slightly more frequently than white, Asian and other families (44 versus 20 per cent).

The reasons for liking the preferred school also varied in terms of family structure. However, given the very small numbers it is really only possible to look at the frequencies for the mother and father families (N = 41), the lone-mother families (N = 16) and the mother and partner families (N = 8). Nevertheless, for the mother and father families the key reasons to emerge were subjects/facilities (46 per cent) followed by academic results (29 per cent) and first impressions (27 per cent). On the other hand, for the lone-mother families subjects/facilities (44 per cent) were followed by the atmosphere (38 per cent) then the environment/buildings (31 per cent).

There were some statistically significant results between parents from different social classes or occupational groupings. More parents where the father was from a non-manual, rather than a skilled manual or semi-skilled/ unskilled social background, liked the school(s) they were applying to because of the environment or buildings (33 versus 5 and 13 per cent). It is also interesting to note that more parents where the mother was from a professional/managerial/technical background than from other non-manual or manual occupational backgrounds liked the school(s) they were applying to because of the way in which teaching was organized (24 versus 3 and 0 per cent).

We have also looked at these reasons for liking the preferred school by the two London boroughs and found that discipline is mentioned somewhat more frequently (but statistically non-significantly) for parents in Wandsworth than in Camden (29 versus 14 per cent). In the next chapter we explore in more depth what parents might mean when they talk of discipline. We also found that environment/buildings are more important to parents in Wandsworth parents than Camden (29 versus 14 per cent). Subjects/facilities were slightly more important for parents in Wandsworth than Camden (53 versus 31 per cent).

In addition to trying to summarize parents' reasons, we looked at the kinds of comments made about the preferred school. We shall return to look at some of these, particularly that of 'discipline' mentioned in the first quotation below at a later stage in Chapter 6. However, it is important to note here a flavour of these comments which included:

It's got a nice old-fashioned feel about it. A bit more discipline which I delight in. It has an excellent exam track record and we were impressed with the facilities at the school.

The quality of the art work, the locality, the positive attitude of the head of Year 7 in terms of the positive attitude at transition . . . and it's a mixed race school as well as mixed gender which we wanted.

First impressions, people were there to welcome you, students included. Pleasant.

If we compare the findings presented in Table 5.3, which give the reasons why parents were thinking about particular secondary schools, we can see that there were references by over one in ten parents to the school being 'new', 'exciting' and 'well resourced'. These were references to the city technology college in Wandsworth; one of the parents for whom this was the preferred school commented:

It was unbelievable, it was like going into a school for the year 2050. It's just a whole new concept of schooling which I love. [Emma's] particularly academic . . . the sports equipment, the equipment, the work stations, the language labs. It was amazing.

Parents were also asked whether they and their child's other parent (or significant adult) agreed about the choice of school. In 81 per cent of families they agreed, while in 1 per cent they disagreed; in 1 per cent the choice was said to be the child's. In 15 per cent of the families, however, the question was not applicable; for example, there was no contact with the other parent and this, of course, applied mainly to the lone parent families.

Choice or Compromise?

We asked parents if they felt that they had had to compromise at all over their choice of secondary school, or were quite happy about the school(s) that they had applied to. Seventy-seven per cent were 'quite happy' while almost a quarter (23 per cent) felt that they had had to compromise. Those who felt that they had had to compromise were asked which school they would *ideally* have chosen and what in particular they liked about this school. Of the sixteen parents who felt that they had had to compromise, nine mentioned that they liked the academic results of the school they would ideally have chosen, five that they liked the atmosphere or ethos, three that they liked the staff/ headteacher, subjects/facilities or discipline. One or two mentioned a range of other reasons such as, for example, that it was a local school, or that they liked the environment/buildings.

Given the emphasis on parental *choice*, the fact that almost a quarter of parents actually preferred a school other than the one they had opted for may be quite significant and a relevant factor in the debate about the alternatives on offer in particular parts of the country. It also means that parents feel rather constrained in what they can actually apply for, as opposed to what they would really like, illustrating the fact that whatever changes towards 'consumerism' or a market in education had occured they had not yet been fully achieved to the satisfaction of all parents in this sample.

The various reasons that the parents gave for not applying to this 'ideal' school were either that they were unable to afford the private school fees (five parents) or that they had applied but there was no place (four parents) and a number of other reasons mentioned by only one parent, such as the school admissions' criteria stipulated that the child must be a Roman Catholic or that the journey to the school was too long. All of these reasons show that *choice* is a complex matter and is not easily arrived at or satisfied. These are also some of the negative reasons that parents invoked about particular schools or rather they may be associated with negative reasons, which do not only have to do with the elusive concept of discipline. We will discuss this in greater depth in Chapter 6.

Factors Important in Choice

We later asked parents a series of questions concerned with factors that parents might have felt were important in their choice of secondary school for their child. The first question involved the interviewer repeating back to the interviewee those factors mentioned in the two earlier questions, and then asking whether there were any other things they felt were important in their choice of secondary school for their child. We then categorized the parents' replies. Table 5.6 gives those factors mentioned by over 5 per cent of the sample of parents.

The three factors, spontaneously mentioned most frequently as important in parents' choice of secondary school, were what we have called the three 'Ps': *performance* (good academic results), a *pleasant feel* (atmosphere/ethos) (each mentioned by about a third of parents) and *proximity* (location: near to home) (mentioned by about a quarter of parents). The subjects offered, facilities and 'discipline' were also mentioned by a significant proportion of parents (this latter issue of 'discipline' is a point to which we shall return in Chapter 6).

We found some interesting differences between the parents of girls and boys. There was one statistically significant result; more parents of boys than girls mentioned that an important factor in their choice of a secondary school was that they liked what they saw (22 versus 0 per cent). Moreover, there was a trend for more parents of girls than boys to state that the school being *single-sex* was important (24 versus 6 per cent). This chimes with earlier findings

Table 5.6: Factors spontaneously mentioned as important in choice of school

Factors important in 'choice'	Percentage of parents (N = 70)
Good academic results	34
Atmosphere/ethos	31
Near to home	26
Subjects offered	23
Facilities	19
Discipline/behaviour	16
Teachers/headteachers	14
Single-sex	14
Good education	13
Liked what saw	11
Child wants school	11
Caters for special needs	10
Good reputation	10
Small school	7
Uniform	7
Mixed school	6
Extracurricular activities	6
Suits child	6
Teacher–pupil relationships	6
Multi-ethnic/cultural aspect	6

about single-sex schooling for daughters. It is also interesting to note that in Camden nine parents (25 per cent) felt that single-sex schools were an important factor, whereas there was only one such parent (3 per cent) in Wandsworth.

No statistically significant differences between parents from different ethnic groups emerged. However, there was a trend for more white and Asian than black parents to mention that the ethos/atmosphere of the school was an important factor (38 or 25 per cent versus 0 per cent) and more white than black or Asian parents mentioned proximity to home (32 per cent versus 11 and 0 per cent). In terms of social class we identified two main differences. First, significantly more parents, where the father was from a non-manual rather than a skilled manual or semi-skilled/unskilled occupation, indicated that the atmosphere/ethos, one of our three 'Ps' — pleasant feel, was an important factor in their choice (53 per cent versus 27 and 0 per cent). Second, there was a trend for more parents who were in traditional family situations than those in lone mother or non-traditional family households to mention that the teachers/headteacher were an important factor (29 per cent versus 6 and 0 per cent) in their choice.

We then read out a list of factors that past research has indicated are sometimes mentioned as important for parents when choosing secondary schools. We asked parents if each of these had been an important factor for them in making their decision about a secondary school for their child. Table 5.7 gives factors that 90 per cent or more of the parents said were important in their choice of school for their child.

It is important to note the range and variety of factors that the majority of

Table 5.7: Prompted factors mentioned as important in choice of school

Prompted factors important in 'choice' of school	Percentage of parents (N = 70)
Good quality education	100
Encourages responsible attitude to school work	100
Pleasant atmosphere	99
Good competent teachers	99
Good discipline	99
Well-organized school	97
Classes well organized	97
Pupils stretched academically	97
Good choice of subjects	96
Good teacher–pupil relations	96
Caring friendly teachers	96
Well-behaved children	96
Pleasant environment	96
Well-managed school	94
Child wants to go	93
Easy to get to	91
Mix of pupils from different social backgrounds	91
Suits child's needs	90
Good computing facilities	90
Good reputation of school	90

parents thought were important to 'choice' of school. Most of these are clearly very positive reasons such as 'good quality education' and 'pleasant atmosphere', whereas others may well be less positive and tending towards the negative, reasons such as 'good discipline' or 'strict rules', factors that we shall explore in greater depth in the next chapter.

We then asked parents which were the three most important factors in their choice of secondary school for their child. This was an open-ended question and responses were categorized *post hoc*. The most important reason for 16 per cent of the parents was the school's academic record or results, one of our 'Ps', performance; for 11 per cent it was the fact that their child wanted to go to the school and for the same percentage of parents it was getting a good education.

A wider variety of reasons was given as the second most important reason; 13 per cent referred to the school's academic record or results again, the performance factor; 7 per cent mentioned the pleasant feel — our second 'P' — and the same percentage of parents cited the wide range of subjects available. A similarly wide variety of reasons was given as the third most important reason. Sixteen per cent mentioned good pupil–teacher relations and 10 per cent mentioned discipline; 6 per cent mentioned the school's academic record and the same proportion mentioned that it was near to home.

As a number of the factors that parents gave us as their first, second and third most important reasons were so diverse, we decided to examine them rather more broadly. Table 5.8 presents the percentage of parents giving these factors as one of the three most important reasons. Using these categorizations, it can be seen that educational factors are most frequently given as the most

Table 5.8: Three most important reasons for 'choice' given by parents

Most important reasons	First most important Percentage of parents (N = 70)	Second most important Percentage of parents* (N = 70)	Third most important Percentage of parents* (N = 70)
Academic record/good education	27 (1)	16 (2)	10
Child's wishes/happiness	20 (2)	10 (3)	13 (3)
Location	14 (3)	9	6
Organization of school	13	29 (1)	25 (1)
Atmosphere/ethos	9	9	4
Type of school (e.g. single-sex)	9	9	10
Discipline	4	7	10
Know school	3	3	3
Recommended	1	—	—
Staff/staff–parent relations	—	7	17 (2)
Reputation	—	3	3

Note: * Percentages do not add up to 100 because of rounding.

important reason, followed by the child's wishes or a consideration of her or his happiness. In other words, slightly over a quarter of our sample of parents gave educational reasons as their main reason for 'choice' but one in five of the parents gave consideration first to their children's happiness or wishes, which may or may not have been in conjunction with their children. In relation to the second and third most important reasons, organizational factors were mentioned most frequently, with educational factors again emerging as important and another factor was highlighted, namely the staff at the school.

For all three questions relating to the three most important factors, a wide variety of reasons emerged, in varying combinations. We did not try to analyse these reasons in any more detail because the diversity is far too great. However, we did look at the kinds of statements made and the range of responses is typified in the examples given below. We should stress that these reasons should not be seen in isolation as they were always given in combination.

> First, good facilities — enough books, enough facilities to assist them with learning. Second, well-organized — children should know exactly what is expected of them. Third, good pupil–teacher relations. I think teachers have to actually enjoy teaching.

> Academic record, good school ethos and discipline.

> She wanted it . . . I was impressed with the education and the uniform.

> First and foremost I liked the feel of the school and . . . it is a Roman Catholic school.

> Single-sex definitely . . . the curriculum — good opportunities in sciences and computing; the after school activities . . . things we

Table 5.9: *The reasons parents gave for the target child liking the preferred secondary school*

Reason child liked school	Percentage of parents (N = 69)
Friends going	53
Child liked what was seen on visit	35
Facilities/subjects	26
Siblings there	16
Near to home	9
Did not like alternative	4

Note: * Percentages add up to more than 100 as more than one reason was sometimes given.

wouldn't have dreamed of when we were at school — pot-holing, rock climbing, weekends away. I wish I could go.

Discipline . . . none of the bullying and racist comment and that sort of thing . . . the exam results.

The most important is good exam results . . . Secondly, good teacher–pupil relationships . . . and thirdly, a well-managed classroom, where the teacher is in control of the children and this makes for a disciplined atmosphere where children can learn.

Rebecca liked it and wanted to go there . . . it offered a good range of subjects and it's near to home.

The Target Child's Choice from the Parent's Point of View

We also asked parents whether they had talked to their child about which school she or he should go to. Ninety-nine per cent said that they had discussed schools with their child. A total of 83 per cent of the parents stated that their children wanted to go to the same school as they wanted them to go to. This of course relates back to the discussion in Chapter 3 about the ways in which responsibility for decisions/choice was arrived at in families and particular different types of family. It also relates to what might be considered the processes of decision-making and 'education' within families, whereby parents may come to influence their children's knowledge in subtle and possibly even manipulative ways, so that there then appears to be agreement in the family on particular educational decisions.

We then asked the parents if they knew why their child wanted to go to his or her preferred school. Table 5.9 gives the reasons given by parents for believing that the child liked the school. Over half (53 per cent) of the children were said to want to go to their preferred school because their friends were going there. About a third of the parents (35 per cent) commented that their children liked what they saw on their visit, and around a quarter (26 per cent) said that their children liked the school's facilities/subjects on offer. A further 16 per cent mentioned that siblings were at the school, 9 per cent that the school was near to home and 4 per cent that the child did not like the alternatives.

There was one statistically significant result between the parents of girls and the parents of boys. More parents of boys than girls reported that their children liked the facilities at her or his preferred school (39 versus 12 per cent). In addition, somewhat more girls than boys were said to want to go to their preferred school because friends were going (62 versus 44 per cent) or because it was near to home (15 versus 3 per cent). In other words the boys, unlike the girls, were more concerned about the facilities/subjects, a point to which we shall return in Chapter 8.

There was a marked difference between parents in the two boroughs as to whether parents reported that 'friends were going' was a reason for the child wanting to go to the schools. The difference was statistically significant with two-thirds (67 per cent) of parents in Camden, compared with only just over one-third (39 per cent) of parents in Wandsworth, reporting that their child liked his or her preferred school because friends were going there. In Camden (at least in the areas covered by schools in our sample) there must, we may surmise, be close social networks for the children whereas this appears not to be the case in Wandsworth where the child's choices may have more to do with the new variety of schools. These views may well have also been influenced by the parents as we have already noted.

Conclusions

In this chapter we have explored the kinds of reasons and factors parents offered for their various 'choices' of school, including the schools they *considered* and *preferred*, and those that might be 'ideal'. We have also matched up what the interviewed parent reported that their partner/other parent and target child thought about the preferred or 'chosen' school. What emerges most strongly from all of this is that there is an almost infinite variety of reasons proffered for 'choice' of school, none of which is easily susceptible to summary. We noted at the beginning of this chapter also that the different ways of asking questions elicited different responses. Furthermore, some of these responses seemed to represent parental accounts of their choice decisions as emerging out of a variety of social interactions and considerations, whereas other responses seemed to indicate that a clear-cut rational decision had been made using more individualistic judgments and priorities.

An important aspect of secondary transfer and choice as a *social process* concerned the presence and significance of *existing links* with particular schools. These existing links might refer to siblings or other known children who already attended a chosen school (Table 5.2). Friends who were planning to go to the chosen school featured prominently in the parental responses about why their children had chosen particular schools (Table 5.9). Yet these social links do not feature in the responses to later questions asked about reasons for choices made (Tables 5.6 and 5.8). Similarly *proximity to home* was a significant issue in responses to the earlier questions about reasons for choice (Tables 5.6 and 5.8) but this is not so prominent in responses to the question about reasons why the preferred school was liked.

Other issues that may relate to choice as a social process appear in other responses. Having a particular school recommended, and references to a school's reputation (Table 5.3) are both likely to reflect interactions and discussions with other parents. In this series of questions these two factors appear to be significant only in one table, yet informal sources of information, such as interactions with other parents were clearly significant in other ways in the choice process, as we saw in the material presented in Chapter 4.

Parents also clearly value what they can see with their own eyes in making judgments about particular schools. Feelings about the 'atmosphere' of schools, 'first impressions', the 'environment' (Table 5.5) and 'liking what we saw' (Table 5.3) each feature in response to only one question, but overall, they suggest that direct observations are an important part of the choice process. More specifically *educational issues* also feature in responses to some questions but not others. Academic results and facilities were both significant in Tables 5.3 and 5.5, while staff and teaching only feature prominently in Table 5.7.

The detailed picture of responses is somewhat ambiguous and multifaceted. We have however found that the three 'Ps' are the most frequently occurring collection of reasons offered in summary by the various parents. These are *performance of schools* (academic results), *pleasant feel* (atmosphere/ethos), and *proximity* (near to home/location). These relate to other reasons presented in other research studies as we had surmised before we commenced our study. Indeed, Elliott (1981, 1982) had suggested that there were three Ps that were important reasons. However, his three Ps were slightly different since he mentioned *product*, what we have called performance, and *proximity*, which is the same as ours, and finally *process* or rather the child's happiness. This last factor did not regularly emerge as important over the course of our interviews; although it was quite frequently occurring, it did not predominate in the same way. In our study we have identified some strong associations between context and reasons, for example the gender of the child has a significant impact on some of the reasons and factors offered, particularly around single-sex schools and small school size for daughters and facilities and liking what was seen for sons. We shall now move on to see whether we can also summarize the reasons for not wanting, rejecting or not choosing particular kinds of schools.

Chapter 6

'Discipline' and Parents' Rejection of Certain Schools

Introduction

In this chapter we look at the reasons parents gave for not choosing certain schools and the factors that they felt influenced their rejection of certain schools and certain types of school. We did ask parents specific questions about this and it is not necessarily merely the obverse of reasons that led parents to choose certain options. We may not, however, be able to tap all the negative reasons since it is hard to get parents fully to express themselves, and we certainly are unable to present parents' views of factors, such as the different cultural or social backgrounds, as explicit negative factors.

We look briefly at whether other children in the family, especially older children, may have an effect upon knowledge and views about reputations of schools. We also explore in more depth what parents meant when they said they did or did not choose a school on the grounds of its 'discipline', an issue that was frequently raised in the interviews either spontaneously or through prompting by us. Indeed, we felt that this emerged as one of the strongest themes related to factors affecting choice of school. However, it was a rather difficult theme to analyse and is certainly not susceptible to quantitative analysis alone. We present our more discursive and qualitative analysis of 'discipline' and how parents understood this notion in this chapter.

About three-quarters of the parents said that there were schools they did not want their child to attend. The most frequently mentioned reasons were poor discipline/behaviour, the school's bad reputation and that they disliked what they saw. First, we will look at the reasons for not choosing or even for rejecting certain schools and then we will move on to our discursive analysis of the concept of 'discipline'.

Schools Parents Did Not Want Their Children To Attend

Information was sought about schools that the parents would really not want their child to attend. We felt that this question would give us some indication

Table 6.1: *Number of schools not wanted*

Number of schools not wanted	Percentage of parents* (N = 70)
None	23
One	36
More than one	26
All borough schools	4
All borough schools except one applied to	9
Do not know/will not say	3

Note: * Percentages do not add up to 100 because of rounding.

Table 6.2: *Parents' reasons for not wanting certain schools*

Reason school(s) were not wanted	Percentage of parents* (N = 51)
Poor discipline/behaviour	51
Bad reputation	45
Dislike what was seen	43
Too far/location	24
Low standards	18
Size of school	8
Threatening atmosphere	8
Drugs	8

Note: * Percentages add up to more than 100 as parents frequently gave more than one reason.

of the 'bottom line' that the parents felt about particular schools and the limits of what they felt their options or choice were. This is at least the obverse of the schools that certain parents felt were 'ideal', but that they were unable to select for various reasons. In particular, we were concerned to know whether or not parents felt that they could easily distinguish between schools in terms of types or other kinds of characteristics. This question did indeed offer us the reverse side of the coin of the positive reasons for choice. Table 6.1 gives the number/type of schools not wanted.

Almost a quarter of the parents (23 per cent) did not name any schools they did not want their child to attend; just over one-third (36 per cent) named one school and almost two-fifths (39 per cent) named more than one school. In other words, almost a quarter of our families did not express dissatisfaction about the range of schools on offer, whereas almost two in five parents were dissatisfied about several of the possible schools. The vast majority of parents (75 per cent) could name schools available that they did *not* want their children to attend.

Those parents who named schools that they did not want their child to attend, were asked for the reasons why these schools were not wanted. Their responses were categorized and those mentioned by 8 per cent or more are shown in Table 6.2. Over half of the parents who had named schools that they did not want their children to attend mentioned as the main reason the poor *discipline* at the school(s), and almost half mentioned the *bad reputation* or that they disliked what they saw. In other words, they would want to reject certain schools.

Around a quarter of the parents did not want a particular school because it was too far away (its location), that is the obverse of proximity. In other words, one of the three Ps was also a factor associated with negative reasons for choice. However, poor discipline and/or bad reputation are not necessarily the obverse of performance or results or even atmosphere/ethos (what we have called pleasant feel) but are possibly independent factors. On the other hand, poor discipline/behaviour and/or 'bad reputation' may lead to the school not having a pleasant feel, or atmosphere. Given that poor discipline/behaviour was mentioned by a majority as a reason for *not* opting for a school, it seems to us to be a significant issue which we will explore in greater depth below. Interestingly, these reasons that parents gave for not wanting a particular school differed by the family relationships to the child and gender of the child. We also explore these factors in terms of social class of mothers and fathers and across the two boroughs.

It is interesting to note that significantly more parents who were lone mothers or in other non-traditional family situations (lone fathers, mother and partner) than those in mother and father situations said that they did not want their child to go to particular schools because they disliked what they saw (64 and 67 per cent versus 25 per cent). In terms of parents of girls and boys, an important and statistically significant result emerged, namely that more parents of boys than girls did not want their child to go to a particular school(s) because of the discipline/behaviour of pupils there (69 versus 47 per cent). In relation to social class differences, significantly more parents where the father had a non-manual than a skilled manual or a semi-skilled/unskilled occupational background, did not want their child to go to a particular school because they disliked what they saw (63 per cent versus 8 and 33 per cent).

It is also worth noting that negative reasons are somewhat differently although not statistically significantly distributed across the two boroughs. In Camden ten parents each mentioned poor discipline/behaviour and a bad reputation whereas in Wandsworth thirteen parents mentioned a bad reputation and sixteen parents cited poor discipline/behaviour. More parents in Camden than Wandsworth mentioned that they disliked what they saw (fourteen versus eight).

In addition to asking why particular schools were not wanted for their children, parents' views on mixed and single-sex schooling in relation to their child were sought. They were asked whether they thought that the fact that their child was a girl or a boy had affected their choice of secondary school. Just over half (51 per cent) felt that it had, 46 per cent felt that it had not and 3 per cent did not know. As we have noted above, the particular reasons parents gave for their preferred school could be distinguished, to some extent, on gender lines.

When asked in what ways they felt it had affected their choice, half of the parents who felt that the sex of the child had affected their choice said that they would like a single-sex school for a girl, but a mixed school for a boy and a quarter said that they would look for different things with a child of the other sex. Indeed, it is the case that far more parents of target girls wanted a single-sex school than for target boys, as we mentioned in Chapters 4 and 5. Curiously, however, parents were more concerned about poor discipline/behaviour and about a bad reputation for sons than for daughters. Comments included:

> I think a boy's got to have a good trade, that's very important. I wouldn't like him to go to an all-boys' school. I'd like him to go to a mixed school.

> He's always been at a coed school . . . I had a sort of feeling, a slight apprehension, about an all-boys' school . . . I think that to go to an all-boys' school you've got to be quite tough. It's the stereotype I have and I don't really want James to be in that situation. I don't see him as a real boys' boy.

> She'd be better without boys around. She'd be better getting on with her school work and then she could cope with boys when she's a bit older.

The child's sex was thus felt to have affected the choice of school for half of the parents. This finding supports that of West and Varlaam (1991) — which was also carried out in inner London — who also found that single-sex schooling for girls was an important factor. We shall return to discuss this as a more abstract issue in the next chapter.

Choice and Other Children

Those parents with an older child (N = 39) were asked whether their experience with their other children had affected their choice; 72 per cent (twenty-eight parents) felt that it had. Half of those (about fourteen parents) reported that they had had a good experience with their older children and were therefore choosing the same school, while *five* parents had had a bad experience and were going to choose a different school. It is not clear though what this 'bad experience' relates to, and whether it is a result of general factors associated with the school, or to other more specific factors in relation to the individual child. Four parents felt that they wanted different schools because the children were different, while three said that they knew the school. A number of other reasons were given by the remaining parents which included, for example, that they knew what to look for.

Parents with a younger child (N = 42) were also asked if their choice of school had been affected by their views about their younger child's education. Over two-thirds (69 per cent) said that it had not, while almost a third (29 per cent) said that it had, and the rest (2 per cent) did not know. Of those who said that their 'choice' had been affected by their views about their younger child's education (N = 12), five indicated that they wanted and had considered a school that *all* the children could go to and the same number felt that if this child got in, the others would follow. Other reasons were mentioned by small numbers of parents, such as not being able to afford private school fees for all the children. This related, as we mentioned in the previous chapter, to some parents' views of an 'ideal' school that was unattainable.

We might summarize these findings by saying that older and younger children did have some effect on the ways in which parents considered various options for schooling. However, there does not seem to be a direct relationship between these reasons and it is not always a negative view of schooling that is reached through older siblings' experiences. On the other hand, younger children may set limits to the range of 'choices' or rather options available to some parents. Again, negative factors are not necessarily paramount.

Discipline — Good Rules or Bad Reputation?

In this section we explore in more depth what the parents actually meant when they talked about ideas to do with discipline. There were clearly a number of cross-cutting issues here since parents were not always only concerned about poor discipline but may also have chosen schools that had good discipline or what others might consider to be quality education. As we have already seen, factors or reasons that parents regard as important for school 'choice' not only have to do with the three Ps (performance, pleasant feel and proximity) and, in particular, the school's examination results or performance but a complex mix of issues such as its atmosphere/ethos or pleasant feel and its facilities. The obverse of these reasons are issues to do with what many parents called 'discipline' and/or 'bad reputation' both of which may be independent factors. What seems to be the case is that parents do refer to the term 'discipline' with great frequency but not with overall consistency.

> Besides education, you should have personality along with — and that you know how to behave. If someone has got so much education and he is not well-behaved that doesn't count. (Mother)

What do parents actually mean by discipline? Discipline is a 'buzz' word — it seems to be a 'noise' that people refer to approvingly but how do we explore its meanings? Mothers may at times say that they 'believe in discipline', assuming that this requires no further explanation or elaboration (Ribbens, 1994 forthcoming). Indeed, Newson and Newson (1965) suggest that discipline is central to motherhood. In other words, discipline here is about setting rules and boundaries to children's behaviour. Or is this what all mothers/parents mean? Approaching the issue from another direction, it raises the central sociological/philosophical issue of social order (in the Hobbesian sense) and how it is achieved by means of ensuring that people learn to accept social rules and norms to avoid social chaos.

On the prompted list of features that people might think important in 'choice' of school, every parent interviewed indicated that good discipline was something they would consider important. They were then asked what 'good discipline' meant to them, as an open-ended question. Responses were transcribed in full and analysed for themes. Answers were then coded under these themes. Each person's answer could be classified under several themes. There were marked contrasts in the answers given, that is, the word could be used to mean very different things, even though everyone agreed that it was important. For example, contrast the first two quotations with the last two:

Good discipline? Attitudes basically. Teachers to children.

Children with problems may need help and it's expensive.

These days there doesn't seem to be enough discipline . . . I mean, there are rules in this life, and the things you learn in school, the respect and discipline, are what get you through adult life I think.

To me, discipline means that if a child is even going to attempt to be out of order, that the child straightaway gets dealt with.

There were definite differences of emphasis between the various themes that emerged from the analysis; for example, is discipline about deference to authority *per se*, or rather is it about being able to move children towards educational goals? As an instance again, it is possible to contrast the first set of quotations, which are largely about deference to authority, with the second set, which focus more on educational goals:

Respect, um, basically you just expect, you know, you expect respect from the children, and they behave themselves, and do as they're told really.

It means that, um, I wouldn't expect my boy to be rude in any way to a teacher. Right. I expect him to, basically, as long as what the teacher asks him to do is reasonable, within the rules, you know, and is not going to, endanger, endanger his safety, that he should do what the teacher asks him.

In a classroom situation? Put it like this. When we were looking around we could go into any classroom as you can, interrupt the class as strangers walking in will do, and whoever was teaching could stop teaching the class, come and talk to the parents, and the class would get on with what it was doing . . . [school Y] there it could not be said. Now is that discipline or is it quality of education or is it merely the teacher enthusing the children enough so that they are quite happy to get on with what they have been told to get on with even if the teacher isn't right there standing over their shoulder? I don't know.

I suppose the main thing is that the children are able to get the most out of the education that they are supposed to be getting in the school.

Considerable concerns were expressed by the parents about observed behaviour but there were many variations between concerns with classroom behaviour, playground behaviour or out-of-school behaviour. For some, it was not any specified aspect of behaviour:

Father: Behaviour really is the main thing.
Mother: And good manners.
Father: Behaviour and good manners.

This corresponds to what Ribbens (1994 forthcoming) found in general terms talking to mothers of primary school children about bringing up their children:

Sally: The main thing is being firm enough.
Jane Ribbens: About any particular issues?
Sally: Behaviour really. (Ribbens, 1994)

Ribbens concluded that mothers could not always specify particular behaviours that were considered 'bad' or 'good' because what was at stake was not any particular aspect of behaviour. Rather, mothers felt they were simply expected to be able to control their children *per se*; the form of behaviour as such would be contingent upon the situation at the time. In other words, mothers felt they should be able to control their children as an indication to others of their good intention to teach social acceptability to their children.

For some, then, in our present study, discipline implied that children should know and exhibit *appropriate* behaviour, however defined. Others, however, did define particular behaviours as significant and therefore relevant or appropriate, especially 'rowdiness', swearing and drugs. There were then great varieties of meaning behind the concept of 'discipline' in these parents' responses, with subtle but very significant contrasts. If we turn to consider the actual distribution of concerns, we find that about a third (34 per cent) of the parents interviewed were concerned with children's attitudes to authority/deference to authority, whether to teachers in person, or to abstract rules:

I don't think there's enough of it in this day and age. When I was at school, you respected your teachers.

Respect, um, basically you just expect, you know, you expect respect from the children, and they behave themselves, and do as they're told really.

Almost two out of every five (39 per cent) of the parents discussed issues of punishment, but, perhaps significantly, only one parent specified corporal punishment as desirable:

I believe in corporal punishment, but there you go. I'd flog 'em. I got it when I was at school. It didn't do me no harm. (Father)

A quarter (24 per cent) of parents spontaneously spoke, on the other hand, of their opposition to corporal punishment:

I'm extremely opposed to corporal punishment, you can put that quite a lot of times! No one touches him.

Many parents were very concerned about how to define appropriate levels of punishment:

I don't know, I mean, although they say it's discipline sending them out of the room, I mean it's not really, is it? I mean, discipline as far as I was concerned was a lot more strict than it is now. I think it's a lot different to what I would imagine. Um. I mean, our teachers were downright rough with us and you got pushed and pulled and teachers got away with a hell of a lot but that was discipline when you were caught and you deserved it. Well, now, I mean, the thing is, if she went to school and the teacher was really strict with her I'd go round there, you know, so it's one of those things, I don't know what to say. You know, it's, I don't know. Um, not taking any nonsense from her basically and making sure she does her homework. Things like that but actually as far as controlling them or punishing them is concerned I wouldn't — things are so different now, I wouldn't know. Until she gets in that environment.

It is interesting to note here that the ambivalence about very 'strict' forms of punishment related to a daughter, whereas a firmer approach to strong discipline was made by a father about his son. A few parents stressed that expectations and rules should be followed through and enforced, whereas other parents again seemed to see the issue almost as one of an outright power struggle, such that teachers should have the upper hand:

And that the teachers sort of over-power the child as such.

By contrast, other parents took the view that bad behaviour should lead to a search for its causes:

Children with problems may need help and it's expensive.

Other parents again felt that it was more a question that teachers should never get to the point of there being bad behaviour or a power struggle in the first place, holding children's attention through their good teaching:

I suppose what I feel is that, that good discipline is somehow the wrong way of coming about it because if there is really good interesting teaching, you know, then you don't necessarily need the same heaviness around shutting up, being quiet and concentrate and part of that is to do with boredom, lack of interest being fired properly . . . basically it's asking for a lot of inspired teachers . . . All I really want is some inspired teaching that, that generates interest from kids without the need, you know, of rules and force and pressure.

. . . a good teacher . . . can hold the children's attention without using force . . . he [sic] should be able to keep that classroom, I'm not saying like mice, but discipline without resorting to [physical means].

Some parents seemed to take this focus on the teachers' obligations further:

. . . The attention [teachers] give to the needs of the children.

Being kept an eye on so they're not getting out of school without anyone even realizing.

A different sort of discussion by some parents stressed the responsibility and cooperation of all school members together so that, for example, children should learn self-discipline and responsibility. Others, over one in ten (13 per cent), also stressed the importance of home–school cooperation and continuity. For over a quarter (27 per cent), peer relations were specified as a particular concern, especially issues of bullying.

Having conducted this analysis of the range and distribution of meanings surrounding 'discipline' we then did a further investigation by reference to the sex of the child under discussion. (This could only really be done where there were sufficient numbers who discussed a particular issue, of course.) In several areas, the sex of the child did not seem to be relevant at all to the discussion; in particular, parents who referred to the importance of rules were equally divided between parents of boys and girls. Despite our above quotations, those who specified their opposition to corporal punishment were slightly more often parents of boys than girls (ten parents of boys, seven parents of girls) but this may have been because corporal punishment in the home is more likely now to be used against boys than girls.

Two areas did, however, seem to show a clearly different pattern according to the sex of the child (although the numbers concerned are too small to be treated as anything more than suggestive). It seemed to be parents of boys who were more concerned about attitudes towards work (eight parents of boys, two parents of girls), particularly wanting schools to help enforce the completion of homework (four parents of boys, one parent of a girl). This mother specifically discussed this issue during another section of the interview:

> [My daughter] she's always got on with the work, but with him it's a constant battle so I do worry more about him. He has to be pushed all the time, and that really worries me.

Similarly, another mother discussed at several points in the interview her difficulties in getting her son to do his homework, and she had used a private tutor at times as a way of ensuring he did some work outside school. She was, therefore, particularly in favour the longer school day at the CTC school:

> ... And one thing I like the best is the longer school day, and the children have to finish everything, all their homework there. That is one of the good things I think, the children have to do there the homework. Whatever they like, after they finish their homework, whatever they like they can do, play or whatever.

While concerns with homework and attitudes towards work seemed to particularly concern the parents of boys, obedience/behaviour seemed to be more often the concern of parents of girls (nine parents of boys and fifteen parents of girls specifically mentioned these issues in general terms). Again, numbers are too small to be at all conclusive, but these patterns are perhaps what one would expect to occur around gender dimensions.

Overall, then, it is very clear that the word 'discipline' encompasses a great range of different meanings, with

- different *areas of concern*,
- great contrasts around the sort of *teacher–pupil relationships* envisaged, and
- different views as to the *purposes of discipline*.

Parents will thus identify, and be looking for, different things in a school or classroom when they say they are concerned with good discipline or decide not to choose a school because of the poor discipline.

In the end, we are left to ponder whether parents here, and elsewhere, are more concerned about social order as a matter of a 'social contract', or a matter of 'social' control of subversive natures. Certainly it appears from the responses we received to be the case that parents were relatively evenly divided on these two matters. Much depends upon their wider social and political views as well as their own upbringing and how they have 'chosen' to bring up their children. We will discuss some of these issues in the next chapter.

Distribution of Responses on the Issue of Discipline

1 *Punishments*
   a Corporal punishment specified   1 (1%)
   b Punishment referred to without discussion of its severity   4 (6%)
   c Punishments and rules mentioned but with qualifications/
      concerns about appropriate levels   22 (31%)
      Of these twenty-two
         No corporal punishment was specified   14 (20%)
         Rejection of corporal punishment specified   3 (4%)
   In total, corporal punishment rejected by   17 (24%)
2 *Authority*
   a Rules   14 (20%)
   b Obedience/behaviour   24 (34%)
   c Respect/manners/no cheekiness   22 (31%)
3 *Control*
   a Control/strictness by teachers   8 (11%)
   b Stressed achievement/enforcement of expectations   4 (6%)
4 *Areas of concern*
   a Peer relations, especially bullying   19 (27%)
   b Attitudes towards work, especially homework   10 (14%)
   c Classroom behaviour   9 (13%)
   d Other aspects of specified behaviour   8 (11%)
      (dress, punctuality, swearing, drugs, truancy)
5 *Pupils, teachers, parents*
   a Responsibility, self-discipline   6 (9%)
   b Parental involvement   9 (13%)
   c Discussion/explanation/respect/attention from teachers
      to pupils   5 (7%)
   d Inspired teaching, educational standards   4 (6%)
6 *Others*
   'Assertive, straight, do good'
   'Treat others as you want them to treat you'
   Ethics/morality
   Flexible rules
   Lenience
   Helping

7   *Analysis by gender of child*

No corporal punishment	10 boys, 7 girls
Rules	7 boys, 7 girls
Obedience/behaviour	9 boys, 15 girls
Attitudes towards work	8 boys, 2 girls
Of these 10 children, homework specified	4 boys, 2 girls
Responsibility/self-discipline	2 boys, 4 girls
Parents should be involved	5 girls, 2 boys

Conclusions

In this chapter we have explored the various factors that led parents to reject, or not to consider, certain schools as options. We were concerned to tease out here whether or not parents felt that they had realistic alternatives in terms of being able to reject certain types of school or schools with particular types of social or other characteristics (e.g. mixed or single-sex schools). We have found that parents did, on the whole, have a view of what kinds of school or what kinds of features of school were unacceptable. In other words, it seems that parents do feel that there are features that distinguish between schools and that not all schools are the same. However they do not necessarily feel that any school matches up to an 'ideal'. In Chapter 5 we saw that only a very small minority thought of an ideal, and that was largely in terms of examination results, and not necessarily a feasible option for the parent in question.

Where schools were not considered appropriate, parents very often raised the issue of poor discipline or a bad reputation. We therefore considered in some depth the ways in which parents conceptualized the notion of discipline. In many respects, parents not only used the term with respect to 'lack of discipline', but also considered it a wider matter of how they and teachers/ schools found ways of controlling or expecting 'good behaviour' from children. We put this section here, however, because in common parlance the term 'discipline' has rather negative overtones. However, we conclude here that some concept of 'discipline' or rather the wider matter of social order and control concerns *all parents* and indeed schools. What it means to parents varies considerably and may depend upon their views and values about society as well as education and children's upbringing.

We turn now, therefore, to these wider questions of how parents considered their children's upbringing and gave expression to their children's schooling where they found it related to their own.

Chapter 7

Choice in a Broader Context of Family Life: Memories, Attitudes, Hopes and Expectations

Introduction

In this chapter we move on to consider the ways in which the families in our sample made their 'choices' from amongst a range of wider factors and contexts. We consider their views of their own education and that of their partners and whether or not it impinged upon their specific decisions or their processes of reaching a 'decision'. We were especially interested in whether or not attendance at particular types of school, such as private or state, religious or not, single-sex or mixed schools, had influenced their views as adults. We were also interested in whether or not their own experiences as pupils or students were at all influential. Of course, we were aware that not all of our sample had comparable educational experiences; for example, several of our parents were the first generation in Britain and might not feel that their own education was comparable with that in Britain, despite the fact that their education might have been British colonial education in India, Pakistan, Africa, Jamaica etc. We were also interested in exploring what the parents' hopes and expectations were for their children's education beyond secondary schooling, and whether or not that might influence the ways in which they thought about the types of secondary schools to which they would send their children. A number of questions were asked about these issues and the answers are analysed and presented in this chapter.

We also consider the parents' general 'political' views about different types of education, such as comprehensive schools, private and/or independent schools, single-sex education and so on. Given that we had selected two boroughs with widely different political positions on education and one that is in the vanguard of changes towards greater diversity of school provision, we were interested to explore the effects of this on a sample of their parent populations. Answers to these issues are also presented here.

Through this wider exploration of contexts and broader issues we hope to reach a clearer picture of the complexity of factors that are habitually taken into account both in the processes of considering schools and school transfer. We also hope to put a better gloss on the fact that secondary school transfer might be considered to be just one factor amongst many that parents take into account in the process of bringing up their children and in the complexity of processes that they consider as 'education'.

Memories of Old Schooldays

We wanted to obtain some sense of whether or how choices about schooling operate within a time perspective that is much greater than just the last year or so of the child's primary school life. We have already seen, in Chapter 4, that there were clear differences between the parents about when they first began to think about secondary schools, although that question might have been interpreted differently by the parents as meaning in terms of particular schools rather than secondary schooling in general. We also wanted to add to our picture of the whole process of thinking about schooling by getting parents to reflect upon their own schooling in relation to their children's. Towards the end of the interviews we therefore asked three open-ended questions about the parents' memories of their own schooldays. The first two of these questions asked the interviewee whether there was anything in particular from their own school experiences that they would want to be different or the same for their children now. The third asked whether the interviewee thought that the school experiences of the other parent had affected her/his views about the type of school the child might attend. Overall, these questions produced some interesting and relevant discussions, which add flesh to our other accounts.

In five of the interviews there were two adults present answering the questions, giving a total of seventy-five possible answers. However, answers were not given to these questions in seven of the interviews. In six cases these were interviews with ethnic minority parents, sometimes with language difficulties in the interview, and in one case the interview was with a grandmother who felt her own schooldays were too long ago to be used as a point of comparison.

In another seven interviews, either the interviewee or the other parent had been educated in a country other than Britain, and this led to perceived difficulties in making comparisons with the child's present school experiences. Of these seven, three had been educated in European countries other than Britain, one in Northern Ireland, two in the Indian subcontinent, and one in Australia. There were only two cases where the interviewees felt that it was difficult to make any comparisons from the past to the present because the child was a different person anyway:

our children are not us, so in a sense there is nothing of significance that I would point at and say, 'Oh gosh! I hope that's different'. (Mother)

So for most people, the questions clearly made sense, and their own school experiences were considered relevant to the choices being made for their children. As might be expected, this could work in both directions, with either good memories they wanted repeated, or bad experiences they wanted to be different for their children (and, of course, the question we asked about siblings was intended to elicit similar kinds of views about whether experiences could be an indicator of the adequacy of schooling).

Memories of schooldays evoked some strong responses with considerable feeling. One woman remarked immediately upon being asked to consider her own school experiences, 'Oh my God!' In one case, the question itself opened up old wounds that the mother did not want to remember:

> well, something bad happened to me when I was young, and they put me in a tiny, a tiny school with only about thirty people there and there wasn't a lot of work being done in the place. So I just hope he gets a better education than I got. It's a part of my life that's sort of dead and buried. (Mother)

In other cases too, there were bad memories of schooldays that parents were anxious not to be repeated for their children:

> my family background was very bad, when I was young, and I know it affected my education very badly, and my personal life . . . I really struggled at my education, and it's just one of those things that no one really took any notice of me. And because the classes were very big, and issues from my personal life outside school affected my school life, I want all the bad things that happened to me, not to happen to my children. (Father)

> I hated school and I wish I hadn't because I feel I would have learned a lot more. Hopefully it's going to be enjoyable enough for her to want to stay. I was forced to go to school, *and hopefully she'll go to the school she wants to go to,* and then she'll enjoy it because it's her choice. (Mother)

> I went to [school X] and I hated school. (Mother)

Altogether, there were *thirteen* parents interviewed (almost one-fifth of those who answered this question) who stated that there was nothing they could remember from their own schooldays that they would want to be the same for their children.

In thirty-five cases,[1] responses were obtained concerning the interviewees' perceptions of how the other parent who was not being interviewed (the father in every case but one) might remember and compare their own schooldays. Out of these thirty-five responses, 17 per cent did not know about the other parent's memories of their schooldays and how this might affect the attitudes to their children's schooling. Eleven per cent said that the father had enjoyed school, although in one case he had not been there very much. Another 11 per cent said the other parent had truanted a great deal, or dropped out (including one mother).

> Unfortunately Mum didn't take to education. She dropped out of education at 13 after several warnings from the various legal departments and she never got back into it again. We are all ambitious for our kids. The majority of people want something better. (Father)

A further twenty-nine said (often in strong terms) that school had been a bad experience for the father — a proportion that seems to suggest a very sad reflection on the fathers' educational experiences.

> Quite bad [experiences] . . . he went to lots of different [schools] . . . It was a single-sex boarding school he was sent to eventually which was his worst experience . . . Totally against boarding schools, private schools. (Mother)

> I think he would probably look for something completely different from what he had . . . he was very determined she shouldn't go to a Catholic school because of his own experiences. I think he was more terrified into learning than encouraged. (Mother)

On a brighter note, there were twelve parents (18 per cent of those who answered this question) who felt that there was nothing about their own schooldays that they would want to be different for their children. For these people, school had been a happy experience that they hoped would be repeated for their children, although not many people expressed it quite as positively as this woman:

> Best years of my life! I thought that every school was the same. I went to a boarding school. It made me confident and there was happiness all around always. (Mother)

Eight interviewees specifically stated their present hopes for their children in terms of happiness when comparing their past schooldays. Mostly these comments were brief references to having been happy at school and wanting the children to feel the same. In two cases, the reverse situation applied:

> I didn't like school. I would like Ben to be happy at school and to like being there. (Mother)

When we come to look at the content of the comparisons being made between the parents' memories of their schooldays and their hopes for their children, the most frequently mentioned topic (referred to by thirteen interviewees) was that of relationships with teachers. Again, as might be expected, this could work in a number of ways. Some were pleased that their teachers had been distant and authoritative, demanding respect, and wanted similar relations for their children, while others wanted teachers to be more open and friendly than they remembered for themselves:

> The thing I liked about the schools, I think all the teachers looked like teachers . . . I think the children could look up to them more . . . some schools expect to be too friendly with the children. (Mother)

> I hope that teachers are more open with children these days. I found the teachers were there from 9 'til 3.30 and that was it, it was just a job, and I hope now they're more friendlier. I mean I couldn't have gone to a teacher with a problem . . . very cold sort of people. (Mother)

Others felt they had been let down by their teachers, with lack of attention and caring, while a few remembered those teachers they had who did show a caring attitude.

The second most commonly mentioned topic was that of discipline, which was referred to by eleven interviewees (we presented a broad discussion in Chapter 6 of the variable meanings of this term). Several people referred to vivid memories of severe corporal punishment. A woman remembered her schooldays in Glasgow thus:

> I mean from the age of 6 I was strapped virtually daily with a leather belt for things like double lines on my dictation or a blunt pencil and, um, and sadistic teachers, six double handers. What they used to do was to put cloths round your wrist because they often split the skin. (Mother)

> Discipline, thank God it's so much different now, I mean, it was so, too physical. I mean, we were beaten at the drop of a hat . . . The cane, you got it for ridiculous reasons like not having a rubber. When you look at it now it was for ridiculous reasons. I'm glad that that stopped . . . that children don't get it, because I was actually — I'm not saying they shouldn't be disciplined, they were just wicked sometimes. Too much of it. (Mother)

Altogether, six people remembered with horror the physical punishments of their own schooldays, and did not want this to be repeated for their children. A further two mothers said the children's fathers had similar memories and attitudes.

On the other hand, in comparing their own schooldays, four people referred to the need for more discipline in their children's schools, although it was clear that only one person was referring to discipline in terms of corporal punishment:

> I didn't get enough discipline. I was a dreamy child, if you are a dreamer you need to be disciplined. (Mother)

> Discipline. There were strict rules, we were very disciplined, if we swore we would be told off or whatever, or sent home, or punishment would be given to us. (Mother, referring to her own schooldays in India).

The topic of single-sex versus mixed schools also received considerable attention in responses to this series of questions, being discussed by ten interviewees in terms of their own experiences, and a further six in terms of the other parent's school experiences. Two mothers had been to mixed schools and wanted their daughters to go to single-sex schools:

> I went to a mixed school which is why she is going to a single-sex school basically. (Mother)

A further two had been to mixed schools and wanted their children (one boy and one girl) to do likewise. Another two had been to single-sex schools and wanted the same for their daughters. The most frequent pattern, however, was for those who had been to single-sex schools to prefer mixed schools for their children; this applied to four people (two fathers and two mothers) being interviewed, and was reported to be the case for a further five parents (four fathers and one mother) not being interviewed. This father expressed his feelings in particularly strong terms:

> Deep psychology here. He's very like me, and I went to a single-sex boys' school and it totally screwed me up . . . I grew up with a most peculiar attitude to women basically because I didn't know any, so it was very important that Andrew should be in mixed company. (Father)

The social life of remembered schooldays was discussed by nine interviewees, almost always in terms of happy memories of friendships. In many of these cases, the social life of school was the one good memory they had that they wanted to be the same for their children.

> Well, socially school was always really important to me. It was my only social life and I always enjoyed school for friends and I think that's the main thing, that he does enjoy school for, it's the only thing that keeps him going . . . it's very important to feel happy socially at school and I'm sure it helps you in every way, academically, whatever, if you feel socially at ease and you've got real friends there. (Mother)

In only one case did the mother remember being unhappy with friendships at school, and hoped her daughter would fare better than she had:

> Hopefully she'll have more friends. In secondary school I found it very hard, they all seemed to form themselves into different groups and if most of them were away you were sort of left on your own. And I think that's sad. I think at secondary school people should be able to mix together and get on. We didn't mix very well. (Mother)

Two people remembered discrimination at school from their peers, one because of disability and one because of race. Nevertheless, for both these people, good friendships had also been an important part of school life. One other mother had unpleasant memories of being bullied at school, and strangely, her daughter had already moved schools during her primary education as a result of bad experiences of bullying.

Six interviewees talked in terms of children being given encouragement, confidence and/or a sense of independence, as something they would want for their children that had been missing for them:

> I'd like them not to tell him he can't — I mean, he already can draw, but if he, if he doesn't show something I'd like them not to say, 'You're never going to be able to do that'. I don't ever want him to feel that he can't do something. It was only two years ago that I got, um, any confidence in maths, because I was told that I couldn't do it. You know, I'd hate anyone to say that to him. (Mother)

> They do have a lot more independence at [my daughter's chosen school] than we had, and they are allowed to make decisions for themselves based upon their own judgments a lot more than ever we were, and I like that much better . . . they seem to be brought up much more to think for themselves, than we ever were. I definitely approve of that.

Only one person remembered being given the positive encouragement she also now wanted her child to be given at school.

So far, then, we have seen that parents gave a lot of attention to the *social relationships* of school life, and its *emotional quality* in thinking back to their own schooldays in relation to what they wanted now for their children. The more strictly *educational* side of school life also received attention from some parents. Seven interviewees discussed the presence or absence of well-qualified and committed teachers in their own school experiences. In five cases, the interviewees remembered having been taught by good teachers, while in two cases there were memories of poor teachers that they hoped would be rectified for their children.

A further six interviewees discussed their own frustrations at not having had the subject choices they wanted at school, or having to make choices too early, a situation that they hoped would be improved for their children — and often felt had indeed improved. Four parents specifically mentioned an emphasis on arts, music or languages as valuable aspects of education that they either had or had not experienced in their own schooling. Specific teaching methods were discussed by five interviewees. This was generally in terms of reading schemes or an emphasis upon 'basics' which they felt had been stronger in the past, but for one woman, it was a memory of boring teaching in her own schooldays that she wanted rectified for her child.

Three interviewees discussed the size of classes when considering their own school memories, with a general preference expressed for small classes. Another three discussed the general environment, buildings and 'atmosphere' of the school as something they remembered with affection:

> My school was lovely you know, a big field, little buildings, and er, when I took [her older daughter] the first time to look [at her secondary school], I had the creeps but she quite enjoyed it, she loves it, the kids don't seem to be bothered by Victorian buildings . . . it doesn't seem to worry them, large size. (Mother)

Four mothers specifically discussed the gender issue in relation to their own memories of school, always in terms of girls not having the same opportunities available to them, or encouragement/expectations put upon them as boys.

The last topic that was frequently discussed, in response to this series of questions, is more difficult to summarize, since it referred to a general feeling about whether or not competitiveness is desirable, and whether or not children should be pushed and stretched educationally. Parents expressed opinions in a variety of directions. Five parents regarded 'stretching' and/or examinations in a positive light, either remembering being positively stretched themselves and/or that emphasis on examinations had been useful; some felt that the standards expected had been too low in their own schooldays. Two mothers specifically linked the lack of 'being pushed' to the gender issue. On the other hand, two parents felt there had been too much emphasis on 'the exam conveyor belt':

> From my experience, I was treated as somebody who was there to pass exams, not as an individual . . . I was on a conveyor belt and I do resent that very much. (Father)

This mother spent some time weighing up the pros and cons of competition and an academic emphasis:

> Although I would want a school that had a good academic reputation, I wouldn't want a school that was too competitive as an overriding

ethos. It is a difficult balance to make, but I wouldn't want a school that valued academic achievement exclusively.

[Was that something you experienced in your own school life?]

It wasn't so much that I felt it, so much as talking to other people at my school, and they seemed to feel it made them unhappy. (Mother)

A few parents lamented their own negative attitudes towards education and exams during their own schooldays.

Overall, then, it appears that the vast majority of parents did see it as relevant to compare their own schooldays with their present hopes for their children's education. Memories of school evoked some strong feelings, with twenty-five interviewees (37 per cent of the possible total) either stating there was nothing they wanted to be different, or else nothing they wanted to be the same as they had experienced in their own education.

The *negative* memories of school predominated, however. In looking at the focus for the comparisons being made between past and present, relationships with teachers and discipline were the most frequently cited topics, with some strong feelings expressed against corporal punishment. Mixed versus single-sex schooling was the next most frequently cited point of comparison, followed by social life at school and relationships with peers, and then general encouragement and independence for children. Topics that are more narrowly educational received much less attention, but relevant areas that were discussed were the quality of teaching, subject choices, size of classes, gender issues in relation to opportunities, and competitiveness/stretching of pupils.

Parents' Views, Future Hopes and Expectations for Children's Education

We asked a number of questions about the parents' general attitudes to types of secondary schools, such as the differences between single-sex as opposed to mixed schools, and secular versus religious education for their children. We also asked about their longer-term hopes and expectations for their children such as whether or not they hoped and/or felt that their child would stay on at school past the minimum school leaving age of 16 and whether or not they hoped and/or felt that their child would go to college or university.

First, we tried to establish whether or not the parents had strong attitudes towards single-sex or mixed schools and towards religious schools, given that in the latter case, over half our parents (N = 39) had children in voluntary-aided schools, as shown in Chapter 1. Then we asked for more general comments. Finally, we considered their longer-term views, hopes and expectations of their children's education and their broader political perspectives.

In fact, we found that almost half (47 per cent) of the parents did not have

Table 7.1: *Views of religious schooling by sex of child*

Religious Views	Boy (N = 36)	Girl (N = 34)	Percentage Total (N = 70)
No strong views	18	15	47
Basically positive	9	9	26
Basically negative	8	9	24
Other	1	1	3

Table 7.2: *Parental attitudes to single-sex schools*

Attitudes to Single-Sex Schools	Percentage of Parents (N = 70)
Basically positive	31
Basically negative	24
No strong views	23
Positive for girls	19
Negative for boys	3

strong views about religious schools, despite the fact that almost two-thirds of the children were in schools with formally religious affiliations. Of those who did have strong views, half (N = 18) were 'basically positive' and half were 'basically negative' (N = 17). Moreover, when asked for their comments on this, it was difficult to find any really distinctive factors. About a quarter of the parents said that religious schools were fine if parents wanted them and one in five of the parents said that they preferred that their child should *not* attend such schools. There were no differences between the parents' attitudes to religious schooling in terms of whether the target child was a boy or a girl, as can be seen in Table 7.1.

There were also no differences between the parents in terms of ethnicity of the child and their religious views. One mother said: The comments made varied, however.

I'm not religious. Such schools are OK for those that want them.

On the whole, the parents in our sample did not want such schools for their children at secondary school stage as a strong or central reason for 'choice', although some of the state schools that were preferred were voluntary-aided rather than county schools (as can be seen from Table 5.1 in Chapter 5).

Parents' attitudes to single-sex or coeducational schools were not as evenly distributed as those views of religious schools. Indeed, attitudes to single-sex schools were mainly *strongly* positive or negative with less than a quarter *not* having strong views, as can be seen in Table 7.2. This is also the case for mixed schools, as can be seen in Table 7.3. We asked a very general question about their views that was not linked with the sex of the child. There are clearly differences between parents' attitudes to single-sex schools for girls as

Table 7.3: *Parental attitudes to mixed schools*

Attitudes to Mixed Schools	Percentage of Parents (N = 70)
Basically positive	50
No strong views	21
Positive for boys	16
Basically negative	11
Negative for girls	1

Note: Percentages do not add up to 100 because of rounding.

Table 7.4: *Attitudes to single-sex schools by sex of child*

Attitudes to Single Sex Schools	Boy (N = 36)	Girl (N = 34)	Percentage Total (N = 70)
Basically Positive	7	15	31
Basically Negative	10	7	24
No Strong Views	10	6	23
Positive for Girls	7	6	19
Negative for Boys	2	0	3

opposed to boys; their obverse views on mixed schools for girls as opposed to boys are shown in Table 7.3.

What is particularly striking in these tables is the fact that two-thirds of the parents felt positive about such mixed schools, either as schools *per se* or for boys, whereas only half of the parents felt positive about single-sex schools either as schools *per se* or for girls. When asked for comments the two most frequently mentioned with respect to single-sex, were that they were better for girls (eight parents), and that the parents preferred mixed schools (thirteen parents).

With respect to mixed schools a similar number said that they were better for boys (ten parents) and that 'they were more natural'. One mother of a boy actually commented:

Mixed schools reflect the real world. They are more natural.

Although we did not ask the parents specifically to link their views about single-sex versus mixed schools to the sex of the child, differences emerged that are quite dramatic. These differences in attitudes to single-sex schools can be seen from looking at parents of sons and daughters, although, interestingly, as many parents of sons are positive for girls as parents of daughters are negative for them (seven parents in each case), as shown in Table 7.4.

It is worth noting here that these attitudes are generally similar for parents from different ethnic/racial backgrounds (with seven white parents and five parents of black and Asian children being positive for girls). However, parents of girls and boys seem not to hold consistent attitudes to single-sex and mixed

Table 7.5: Attitudes to mixed schools by sex of child

Attitudes to Mixed Schools	Boy (N = 36)	Girl (N = 34)	Percentage Total (N = 70)
Basically Positive	19	16	50
No Strong Views	7	8	21
Positive for Boys	7	4	16
Basically Negative	3	5	11
Negative for Girls	0	1	1

Note: * Percentages do not add up to 100 because of rounding.

schooling, as can be seen from Table 7.5, where we present their attitudes to mixed schools by the sex of the target child.

There were virtually no differences in attitudes to mixed schools between the parents of boys and the parents of girls, but we can see that parents of sixteen girls are positive about mixed schools and a similar number of parents of girls were found to be positive about single-sex schools, whereas only seven parents of girls were basically negative about single-sex schools or equally had no strong views. Similarly, parents of nineteen boys were basically positive about mixed schools, but only ten parents of boys were basically negative about single-sex schools or had no strong views (ten parents) or were positive for girls (seven parents). In other words, parents do not see their views on single-sex schools as being the opposite of their views about mixed schools. These findings support those made in Chapter 5, namely that single-sex schooling is seen more positively in relation to girls than to boys.

Although it appears that the *majority of parents* hold *strong views* on both types of schools it does not mean that these strong views are held equally. Of course, some parents may feel differently about these schools for sons and daughters and may have children of both sexes in the family. What is the most distinctive factor here, however, is that more parents want single-sex schools for girls than boys and that they want mixed schools for boys, often on the grounds that it is 'more natural'!

We have also already seen that parents' attitudes to types of schooling, including single-sex or mixed schools, are influenced by their own early educational experiences. These apparently contradictory views of single-sex versus coeducation may then be a result — at least partly — of the parents' own experiences rather than a systematic review of the currently available evidence and debates in the media.

These views about types of school may be less important issues for the parents than their longer-term hopes and expectations. We asked parents a series of questions about their child's future education. We found that the vast majority of parents (93 per cent) hoped that their child would stay on at school or in education after the end of compulsory schooling. A large majority of the parents (77 per cent) also thought that the child would stay on after the minimum

Table 7.6: Parental expectations about staying on in education/at school

Think child will stay on	Boy (N = 36)	Girl (N = 34)	Percentage Total (N = 70)
Yes	29	25	77
No	1	1	3
Don't know	6	8	20

Table 7.7: Parental hopes for a university/college education by sex of child

Hope for college/university	Boy (N = 36)	Girl (N = 34)	Total Percentage (N = 70)
Yes	34	24	83
No	1	1	3
Don't know	1	9	14

Table 7.8: Parental expectations about higher education by sex of child

Think child might go to college	Boy (N = 36)	Girl (N = 34)	Total Percentage (N = 70)
Yes	24	20	63
No	3	2	7
Don't know	9	12	30

school leaving age. Similarly, the majority of the parents (83 per cent) hoped that their child would go to university/college and a majority (63 per cent) thought that their child would go to university/college.

Given that 93 per cent of parents hoped that their children would stay in education after 16, it is difficult to distinguish between hopes or even realistic expectations for either sons versus daughters. Perhaps it is slightly meaningful that, of the five children's parents who were not sure whether their child would stay in education after 16, four were girls and only one a boy and, interestingly, all were white families. It is also the case that a quarter of the parents of girls were not sure whether their daughters would stay on, while a smaller proportion of parents of boys were uncertain, as can be seen in Table 7.6. Fourteen of these families were white and two black.

Parental hopes for their children's further or higher education are also very similar in relation to the sex of the target child, except that more parents of girls than boys (nine versus one) were not sure, as can be seen in Table 7.7. Of the families who were unsure, ten were again white and two Pakistani.

Perhaps parental expectations about their children's educational careers were more grounded in reality, as can be seen from Table 7.8, with only about a third of parents (63 per cent) *expecting* higher education and more families with sons than daughters expecting such educational careers. However, the wider evidence now suggests that girls do at least as well as boys in the examinations leading to a higher education career. Out of the twenty-six families that were not so certain, twenty were white, four were black and two were Pakistani.

It is important to note that the families in our sample were, on the whole, hopeful and expectant that their children would have educational careers beyond school. Although we have already mentioned that the sample is skewed towards what we would traditionally term the middle classes and the skilled working class, these figures seem to be greater than one might have predicted, especially in relation to parental hopes. However, we did not probe about what kinds of further or higher education parents were thinking about. It might have been about a vocational or technological career rather than the more strictly academic. Nevertheless, there is strong evidence that parents generally have a positive evaluation of education as a 'good thing'.

Political Values and Attitudes to Educational Policy

We also asked parents a series of questions about parents' attitudes, in general, to different types of school, such as comprehensive schools, grammar schools, LEA schools and private education, and to the assisted places scheme as well as to new types of school. We were concerned with eliciting information on their knowledge of current government policies and their views on the central plank of those policies, namely, choice in education. We also wanted to get a sense of their political opinions and asked about their views of party political positions or policies on education, including their views on the former ILEA. This was in an attempt to locate their views in a wider political context.

We found that parents were evenly divided with virtually half of our parents (47 per cent) having favourable attitudes towards comprehensive schools, and half with unfavourable attitudes (49 per cent) to grammar schools. However, many of the parents were not really sure about the differences, including some white English parents, nor were they clear about the differences between state and private schools. Generally, almost two-thirds of our parents (66 per cent) also had favourable attitudes towards private schools, largely (41 per cent) on the grounds that parents should have *choice*. Most of the specific comments about comprehensive schools tended to be unfavourable, such as saying that they were 'too big'. One mother commented:

> The concept is good but it does not work in practice. It is difficult for teachers with mixed ability range to teach.

A father made more unfavourable comments:

> I don't like the children teaching themselves . . . Don't know enough about it to say more.

Table 7.9: Knowledge of new types of school by LEA

New Types	Camden (N = 36)	Wandsworth (N = 34)	Total Percentage (N = 70)
Yes	10	26	51
No	26	8	49
Total %	51	49	100

Similarly, the specific comments on grammar schools tended to be unfavourable, with a third of parents saying that such schools were 'unfair and/or élitist'. Another mother, who herself went to grammar school, commented:

> They are a bit élitist. It's unfair to judge on the eleven-plus. It's not fair on those who do not make it to grammar school.

But another parent who favoured grammar schools said:

> Because they hang on to the old-fashioned values which is education. (Father)

A slight majority (51 per cent) of parents had heard of the assisted places scheme for children with parents on low incomes to attend private schools, but only a third of parents (30 per cent) thought it 'a good idea'. Another mother commented:

> It's fine if you want to go to a private school. I'm sure it helps. I'm not sure how assisted it is!

About half of the parents (51 per cent) had heard of new types of secondary schools, but only a third (31 per cent) could name city technology colleges, and a meagre 6 percent grant-maintained schools, although a further 10 per cent mentioned both GMS and CTCs, meaning that less than half of the parents actually knew of particular types of new school. And, indeed, as might have been predicted, more had heard about these new types of secondary school in Wandsworth than in Camden, as can be seen in Table 7.9. However, the majority of parents in Wandsworth, who knew about the new types of school only named the CTC, with a smaller number knowing about both CTCs and GMS, and in Camden far fewer parents knew about one or other or both.

We also asked a general question about *how much choice* parents should have in the schools their children attend and whether or not what was available in their LEA at the time was 'about right'. The answers are shown in Table 7.10, which shows that half of the parents were not fully satisfied with the present levels of choice. The comments made ranged from saying that 'the choice should be as wide as possible' (ten) and that 'it should not depend on the distance' (ten) to saying that 'there is no real choice now' (nine). These comments linked with the parents' views of the policies in their LEA and the

Table 7.10: *How much choice parents should have*

Is choice now sufficient?	Percentage of Parents (N = 70)
Want more choice	50
About right	44
Want less choice	6

Table 7.11: *Parental views of the LEA's education policies*

How do you feel about education policies?	Percentage of parents
No strong views	41
Negative feelings	31
Positive feelings	20
Know nothing about	4
Mixed views	3

Note: Percentages do not add up to 100 because of rounding.

amount of choice available. Over a quarter of the parents (26 per cent) were happy with the choices available, and a further 10 per cent actually felt that there was 'a good choice', while over a third (36 per cent) were either unhappy with the choice or 'needed more choice'. For instance, one mother commented:

> There is a reasonable choice. I haven't visited all of them. I don't really know. I can't really comment.

Another parent, this time a father, commented:

> Do they [parents] have a choice at present? I think it's a lottery!

These varied views of the choices of school available link with the parents' varied and mixed views of the borough's education policies in general. These are shown in Table 7.11. It is clear from this table that the majority of parents are what we might consider to be 'apathetic' and not at all interested in politics in relation to education. This is to some extent confirmed when we asked the parents to state whether or not they felt that there had been major changes since the abolition of the ILEA, and a third (33 per cent) felt that the impact was in 'less funding to schools', while one in five felt that there was 'no change' and over one in ten simply didn't know. Of course, one might add that the majority of our interviewees were *women* and in traditional political science literature it has been shown that women tend to be less interested in politics and party politics than men (Lovenduvski *et al.*, 1993).

Moreover, we asked parents whether there were party political education policies with which they strongly agreed or disagreed, and we asked separately about each political party's — Conservative, Labour and Liberal-Democrat —

education policies. For each political party the majority of the parents had no strong views (with 50 per cent having no strong views about the Conservative policies, 60 per cent in relation to Labour policies and over 70 per cent in relation to the Liberal-Democrats' policies). However, almost a third (twenty one) said that they 'strongly disagreed' with Conservative policies while almost one in five (twelve) agreed with Labour education policies. Again, we could surmise that this low level of interest is to do with the fact that the majority of interviewees were mothers. However, this may be at odds with the detailed interest shown in the substance of school choice in the interviews themselves.

Individual Stories

Here we present a number of individual stories from the parents which add to our accounts and show how our particular parents put together their memories, hopes and expectations in order to influence their decisions about 'choice' of secondary school:

Mr and Mrs B had moved to their present address seven years previously, but had decided they did not like the local primary school. Instead they had decided to send their children to [school X], which had been Mr B's own primary school when he was a boy. This school was some distance away in a different borough.

Mrs L lived in a reasonably situated council flat. This interview was a 'cold call' because the family were not on the telephone, but I was very eagerly welcomed in. Mrs L appeared a little nervous about being interviewed, possibly slightly 'in awe', but she was delighted to be included. Her three sons' education had been rather a traumatic story to date. She had originally applied to [school A] for her eldest boy, but the application had been lost and he had been sent to [school B] instead, where he stayed until aged 9. When her second son also started at B, he had been badly beaten by another boy. At this stage, Mrs L had approached the Educational Welfare Officer, and had eventually been able to obtain places for all three boys at A, but only after her youngest child had missed his first nine months of school altogether.

Mrs W lived in a very nicely modernized older terraced house. She had very strong feelings about the school she wanted for her son, and was using all possible means she could think of in order to ensure he obtained a place. She herself had not had much of an education.

> Oh, love, I was expelled! I'm afraid so. There isn't no cane no more, but I did have the cane quite often. [My son's] got entirely different upbringing to me anyway. I was from a one-parent family, my mum worked and I really didn't realize I needed an education. No one ever

encouraged me. My mum never realized I needed an education. I'm 41 now, and when I was younger no one ever made the children do homework, not in my environment anyway. I hope that [my son] goes to school to learn.

Mrs P lived in a 1930s terraced house, at some distance from her son's primary school. Her son had always attended X primary school because it was close to the shop his mother owned. When he first started there, the one child he knew beforehand was the child of a customer in the shop. Now in ill-health, she was hoping to move all her children to more local schools.

Mr E lived in a modern mid-terraced house that could have been a private or council development. A lively man with strong views, he lived in the house with his son, while his wife lived elsewhere with his other two sons. He was unhappy about the options available to his son, which he felt were very limited: 'I am really so depressed at what is available'. One new school he regarded as 'a lot of hype', and objected to what he described as the requirement to spend £200 on the uniform. He felt there had been considerable communication problems with the school attended by his older son, which he described at some length. He had applied to private education for his middle son, even though he disagreed with it on principle, 'but then there is no real choice'.

> As a rule, on one side of the coin, we teach the children of the wealthy to expect the best out of life. Children of the working class are actually imbued with a sense of failure, built-in failure, their limitations . . . My idea is that education is a brilliant experience, it really is, and whether you want to intellectualize about it or whether you want it at a practical level, use it, it will give you the tools and answer so much about life. If you don't get it you are stumbling about in the dark.

Mr S lived in a modern end-terraced house that might have been council or private. A Ghanaian, separated from his English wife, he had particularly strong views on racial issues in education. He had considered private education for his son, even though politically opposed to it. However, he had rejected it because of racial issues — he was concerned that his son would be in a small minority in such a school, and that the composition of the particular school concerned did not reflect the racial mix of its neighbourhood. He also felt that private schools do not deal with racial issues seriously.

Mr and Mrs W were clearly a middle-class couple. They had both been privately educated, and now worked in education and in social services. Mr W regretted that their income was not sufficient to provide private education for their son. Nevertheless, there had been aspects of their own schooling that they had both liked and disliked. They were now torn between choosing the more traditional style of the new grant-maintained school available, and the atmosphere of the local LEA school with its absence of uniform. They thought this school might suit their son's personality better, since it placed emphasis on the arts and music, and seemed not to have too 'macho' a culture.

Mrs K was interviewed at her place of work, a national organization concerned with the well-being of children. She had also been involved in parents' organizations in her local borough, and was thus very well informed. Nevertheless, she found she relied upon reputation, rather more than on exam results.

> Exam results tend to be presented in a fairly incomprehensible way because of the schools, with weighting factors and percentages and so on . . . [school X] tends to present their results in terms of diagrams and percentages so you're sort of slightly not sure what's going on . . . At one point we got all the exam results from the local education department and I passed them on to another parent who put them all on his computer and he said it wasn't all that helpful because some schools were better at one subject than another, so it's not easy to make a straightforward comparison.

We can see from these accounts or individual stories that parents approach the question of choice of school in very different ways depending upon their own biographies and experiences of school. They also use their own particular political values in varied ways, usually as mediated by particular experiences, as can be seen, for example, from Mr S in contrast with Mr and Mrs W.

Conclusions

In this chapter we have explored the wider contexts in which parents were making their decisions about secondary schools for their children. We have looked at whether or not the parents' own educational experiences might have played a part in the ways in which they considered schools for their children. Indeed, we have shown that a range of issues impinged upon the parents from their own educational histories, but, most especially, negative factors influenced how the parents looked at secondary schools. Factors such as relationships with teachers and discipline were the most frequently cited topics, with particularly strong feelings expressed against corporal punishment. Single-sex versus co-education was also a point of comparison for parents, although how it affected parents' views depended upon very particular experiences.

We have also explored parents' current views of types of school, drawing on their own memories, and extrapolating their hopes and expectations for their own children. We have found that the parents' attitudes to types of education, such as religious, single-sex or mixed schools, are not susceptible to easy summary and are not the most important factors that concern parents about secondary schools. However, more parents would opt for mixed secondary schools for their sons than their daughters but more for single-sex secondary schools for their daughters than for their sons, influenced possibly by a lot of the current media attention about such matters, although in inner London almost all the research has shown such preferences (West and Varlaam, 1991; West, 1994).

Parents do, however, have very strong expectations and hopes for their children's educational careers. Almost all of the parents interviewed hoped that their children would remain in school after the age of 16, and, moreover, that they would go on to college or university. These hopes were somewhat tempered by reality, in that a smaller proportion, but nevertheless still the majority, thought that their children *would* stay on or go to college. In other words parents had strong and positive evaluations of education as a 'good thing'.

Finally we explored a range of views about policies on schools and education in order to locate parents' specific 'choices' in a broader context. However, parents on the whole did not have strong views about state versus private education and schools, nor about wider politics in education. It appears that their views on secondary school choice are largely related to their own particular situations and here most parents felt that they had a reasonable set of options about secondary schools and, although they might have liked more, they were either realistic or fatalistic about their chances of having 'more choice' and feeling fully 'in control' of their children's education.

We also put together a picture of the ways in which different families approached the processes of thinking about and coming to some view of particular schools by presenting a series of vignettes or rather individual stories about the diverse processes in which parents engaged.

We turn now to look at the children's own views of their involvement in the processes of choosing a secondary school before drawing together the many threads about the processes of the decisions on secondary schools.

Note

1 In five cases both parents were directly involved in the interview anyway; in other cases, either the other parent had been educated in a different country, or there was no contact with the other parent.

Chapter 8

The Pupils' Stories of Choice

Introduction

In this chapter we consider the children's point of view, drawing on the children's responses to the questionnaires that they filled in at school. All of the 134 children who filled in the questionnaire were the original target children but, given the response rate of our parent sample, almost half of the children's parents had not been included in the previous study analysis. This pupil study, therefore, consists of both the parent sample's children and their classmates who were also asked to fill in a questionnaire. We have an extremely high response rate to this section of the sample. However, we asked a far more limited number of questions here than in the main sample in trying to draw out the pupils' views of the salient features of the process and the schools. We were particularly interested in the schools that the children liked and their reasons for this. Of the 134 pupils who completed the questionnaire, seventy-six (or 57 per cent) were girls and fifty-eight (or 43 per cent) were boys.

Pupils' Preferred School

We asked the children which secondary school she or he would most like to attend. Table 8.1 shows the types of schools that they named.

One-fifth of the pupils reported that they wanted to go to an LEA mixed school and slightly more wanted to go to an LEA girls' school. A boys' school was named by just over one in ten pupils. Under a fifth named a school in another LEA. A grant-maintained school was named by 14 per cent and the city technology college in Wandsworth by 11 per cent.

The vast majority (81 per cent) of the children stated that they and their mother named the same school as their preferred school. Similarly, the majority (62 per cent) of the children mentioned that they and their father named the same school, although the proportion is somewhat smaller than in the case of children reporting that they and their mother named the same school. We can see here the key role played by the mother in conjunction with the child in the choice process.

Table 8.1: *Secondary schools preferred by pupils*

Type of school	Percentage of pupils (N = 133)*
LEA mixed (C/V)	20
LEA girls (C/V)	22
LEA boys (C/V)	11
Out of LEA (C/V)	16
Grant-maintained	14
City technology college	11
Private	7

Note: * N is less than 134 as all pupils did not answer every question percentages do not add up to 100 because of rounding.

Table 8.2: *Factors that pupils think are important in secondary schools*

Factor	Percentage of pupils (N = 134)
Good education	94
Good art facilities	88
Friendly teachers	87
Good science facilities	84
Good computing facilities	84
Good sports facilities	84
No bullying	82
Easy to get to	78
Nice buildings	77
Good canteen/lunches	75
Friends going there	74
Good exam results	72
Good clubs	63
Good music facilities	62
Nice facilities	53
Near to home	53
No uniform	34

This process of deciding on the preferred school within the family was taken seriously and the majority of children had talked with their parents about it. Around one-fifth of the pupils (19 per cent) indicated that they had talked about secondary schools with their parents (or adults they lived with) 'a great deal'. Nearly half (46 per cent) had talked about secondary schools 'quite a lot'. Over a quarter (29 per cent) had not talked very much about secondary schools and 4 per cent had not talked about secondary schools at all with their parents (2 per cent of pupils did not answer the question).

We also asked pupils what sorts of things would make them want to go to a particular secondary school. A list of questions was provided, to which pupils were asked to respond with 'yes', if they felt it would make them want to go, 'no' if they did not feel it would make them want to go or 'don't know' if they did not know. Table 8.2 gives the percentage of pupils who felt that specific factors would make them want to go to a particular secondary school.

Nearly all of the children (94 per cent) felt that a 'good education' would make them want to go to a particular secondary school. Nearly nine out of ten mentioned 'good art facilities' (88 per cent) and 'friendly teachers' (87 per cent) as important factors. Over eight out of ten pupils mentioned 'good science facilities', 'good computing facilities', 'good sports facilities' (84 per cent each) and 'no bullying' (82 per cent). In other words, the vast majority mentioned positive and mainly educational factors as reasons for liking a school. Thirteen per cent of pupils mentioned other things that would make them want to go to a particular secondary school — for example, good language facilities (mentioned by three pupils), 'good fun' (mentioned by two pupils) and a sibling already there (two pupils).

Some interesting differences emerged here between boys and girls with significantly more boys than girls stating that good computing facilities (95 versus 77 per cent), good sports facilities (93 versus 77 per cent), and nice buildings (88 versus 70 per cent) would make them want to go to a particular secondary school. On the other hand, significantly more girls than boys indicated that good music facilities (76 versus 46 per cent) and friendly teachers (93 versus 79 per cent) would make them want to go to a particular secondary school.

There were also some interesting differences between the two boroughs, with significantly more pupils in Camden than Wandsworth feeling that good music facilities (75 versus 55 per cent), no uniform (59 versus 20 per cent) and no bullying (98 versus 74 per cent) would make them want to go to a particular secondary school. However, more pupils in Wandsworth than Camden felt that a nice uniform would make them want to go to a particular secondary school (70 versus 29 per cent). This might link with the different types of school available or the different rules and regulations, at least in relation to school uniform at secondary schools, in Wandsworth and Camden.

More pupils whose parents had not been interviewed than those whose parents had been interviewed felt that friends going to the school would make them want to go to a particular secondary school (85 versus 63 per cent). However, the most frequently endorsed factors that would make pupils want to go to a particular secondary school were a good education, good art facilities and friendly teachers. Good science facilities, good computing facilities, good sports facilities and no bullying were all mentioned by over eight out of ten pupils. Similar findings were also obtained by West *et al.* (1991) in an outer London LEA.

Schools That the Pupils Would Not Like

We also asked the children whether there were any secondary schools they would *not* like to attend. The vast majority (79 per cent) said that there were schools that they did not want to go to. We gave pupils the option of naming up to two schools. About half (52 per cent) named one school that they did

Table 8.3: *Reasons why pupils did not like particular schools*

Reason	Percentage of responses (N = 222)*
Bullying	18
Threatening atmosphere	12
People there/Unfriendly children	12
Too far away	9
Buildings/environment/facilities	9
Mixed	6
Bad reputation	5
Single-sex	5
Others**	24

Note: * This refers to the total number of responses made.
** Other reasons each comprising less than 5 per cent of responses (e.g. uniform, no friends there).

not want to attend and over a quarter (27 per cent) named two schools that they did not like.

We also asked what the pupils did not like about the schools that they said they did not want to attend. Their responses were categorized and Table 8.3 gives the percentage of responses in these categories. Around a fifth of the responses referred to bullying with a threatening atmosphere (12 per cent) and the people there or unfriendly children (12 per cent) also being mentioned relatively frequently. The children's comments included:

The children were not very friendly, and I didn't like the atmosphere.

I don't like the facilities, I think there is bullying there and their music is awful.

It's just dirty and I'm afraid of being bullied.

I think it's too rough (too many bullies).

When pupils' reasons for not wanting to go to particular schools were examined further, it becomes apparent that these are not always based on what they have seen. Rather, a particular school's unpopularity is frequently based on what the pupils have heard about a school. However, this is not always the case. In fact, we were able to discern three main categories of reasons for pupils not wanting to go to a particular school. These were related to first, *direct experience*, usually through visits to the school, second, to a *school's reputation* and third, to the *type of school*. Comments from the pupils indicating that they did not like what they saw on visits included:

The atmosphere is very unfriendly and the children are unwelcoming.

The children there were not very friendly and I didn't like the atmosphere.

The view that these schools had an unpleasant atmosphere is particularly interesting given that a 'pleasant atmosphere' is one of the most important factors for parents when choosing a school for their child. It is one of the three Ps that we have identified. There is a suggestion from the comments made by children about the schools that they did *not* like that the same factors would emerge for children in terms of the schools they *do* like. This issue is one that merits further investigation.

Second, in relation to the 'reputation' of a particular school, the pupils' comments clearly indicate that they too have a 'grapevine', and glean their information about secondary schools from a variety of sources. A selection of the comments that they made are as follows:

In [School X] I heard people smoke and take drugs.

There's low education there. People say it's rough at [School Y].

Because it hasn't got a good education and there is bullying and because I've heard people sell drugs there.

I wouldn't fit in with the crowd. I have heard some bad things about its background which I won't mention.

I think there is bullying and their music is awful.

Although most of the comments were concerned with bullying (18 per cent), the unpleasant atmosphere (12 per cent) and the 'people there/unfriendly children' (12 per cent), some pupils made reference to the type of school or its lack of uniform:

It hasn't got any girls and I would like to meet some new friends. (Boy)

It is just a girls' school. (Girl)

Because they are both all girls' schools and I don't think I would fit in there. (Girl)

Type of School Preferred: Single-Sex or Mixed?

Although we asked the pupils which *named* school they would like to attend, we also asked them a more general question about the *type* of school they

Table 8.4a: Reasons pupils preferred a mixed school

Reason	Percentage of pupils (N = 59)
Friends of both sexes	27
Children should mix	27
Better environment	12
Always been in a mixed school	10

Table 8.4b: Reasons pupils preferred an all girls' school

Reason	Percentage of pupils (N = 29)
Do not like boys	31
Boys tease and/or bully	28
Enjoy it without boys	17
Friends there	17
Work better	14
Parents wanted girls' school	10
More friends at girls' school	10

would like to attend. We asked them whether they would prefer to go to a mixed school, an all boys' school or an all girls' school. While nearly half (44 per cent) of pupils reported that they would prefer to go to a mixed school and a little over one in five (22 per cent) that they would prefer to go to an all girls' school, only 5 per cent indicated that they would prefer an all boys' school. In other words, given that we had seventy-six girls replying, forty per cent or two in five of the girls stated that they would like to go to a single-sex girls' school. The responses to this question do not concur with those to the earlier question, as this question is more abstract and not related to a specific named school, to which they have already committed themselves psychologically. It is, nevertheless, very interesting to note this preference for single-sex girls' schooling.

Over a quarter of pupils (29 per cent) 'did not mind' which type of school they went to. They offered the following kinds of comments:

I don't mind whether it's girls or mixed, it's the education that counts. (Girl)

I don't mind because I just want good GCSE results or A level results. (Boy)

I don't mind, because I will grow up the same which ever I go to. (Girl)

Tables 8.4a and 8.4b give the reasons pupils gave for preferring particular types of schools. We have given those responses mentioned by 10 per cent or more of the pupils.

Over a quarter of the pupils who said that they would prefer a mixed school said that they had friends of both sexes or that children of both sexes should mix (27 per cent each). Comments relating to these two notions included:

I think that boys and girls should get to know each other.

I've been in a mixed school all my life and I don't want to change.

Because you can get mixed up with other boys and girls. (Girl)

I think that a school should be mixed with the opposite sex. (Boy)

Because I don't think it's right to keep boys and girls separate. (Girl)

Because I think that boys and girls should get to know each other. (Boy)

Comments were also made which related to the fact that they had 'always been in a mixed school':

I'm used to girls in the school. (Boy)

Because I've been in a mixed school for a long time and I'm used to it. (Girl)

Because I've been to a mixed school all my life and I don't want to change. (Boy)

Pupils also offered comments related to 'better environment', such as follows:

I'd rather go to a mixed school because I'd fit in and not feel left out. (Girl)

Because I think it's good for girls and boys to work together. (Boy)

Nearly a third of the girls reported wanting to go to a single-sex school because they did not like boys and over a quarter said that boys teased and/or bullied others. Comments included:

I do not like boys and you get picked on.

I would like to go to an all girls' school because I don't get on with boys.

Because boys like to tease you and bully you.

Because boys always bully me and I get shy in front of boys.

They also made comments which related to 'enjoying school without boys':

Because sometimes it's enjoyable without boys!

There were also comments that related to the fact that they 'work better' without boys:

Because I get fed up of boys and I can't concentrate as well with boys.

Finally, they made comments that related to the fact that their parents wanted an all girls' school:

Because my mum says you work better with no boys.

Because I have two brothers and I want to get away from them. Also my mum thinks I'll do better there.

Of the seven boys who indicated that they would prefer a single-sex school, only three were able to say why (better sports, work better, more friends there) and one offered this comment:

Because then boys can get on with their work.

Pupils were also asked whether they would like to go to a religious or church school. Ten per cent said that they would, while the majority (57 per cent) said that they would not like to go to a religious school. About a third (34 per cent) of the pupils said that they 'did not mind' whether the school was religious or not.

The main reason given by pupils for wanting to go to a religious school was that they attended church. They also offered the following comments about liking religious schools:

To learn more about God.

Because I would like to find out more about religion.

The main reasons given by pupils for *not* wanting a religious school were that they were not religious (mentioned by 33 per cent of those who said that they would prefer a non-religious school), that there was too much religion (14 per cent), and that they did not believe in God (8 per cent). The following comments were made about why the pupils would *not* choose a religious school:

Table 8.5: *Percentage of pupils reporting various links*

Links	Percentage of pupils (N = 134)
Other pupils from primary school want to go	84
Friends want to go there	83
Friends go there now	68
Sibling there now	23
Other relatives go there	18
Other relatives used to go there	18
Know someone who works there	14
Linked to church	10
Sibling used to go there	10

Because religion should be out of school and not in it.

Because I have no religion whatsoever.

Because of my religion which is Jehovah's Witness.

Because some people from other schools might cuss you.

Because they do a lot of things that I don't need for my education.

I don't want to pray every day to somebody I don't believe in!

Because you only learn one religion.

Because I have not been baptized.

Finally, comments were offered which expressed the view that the pupils were indifferent to secular or religious education:

Because my mum and dad said they wanted me to make my mind up for myself.

I don't mind as long as I get a good education.

Links with Secondary Schools

Pupils were asked about the links they had with the secondary school they would most like to attend. Table 8.5 gives the percentage of pupils reporting various links. Friends of various kinds — either at the current primary school or older friends — are the main source of links with secondary schools. The social aspect and familiarity of at least some of the pupils at the large and

Table 8.6: *Number of brochures read*

Number of brochures	Percentage of pupils* (N = 131)
None	32
One	24
Two	16
Three	17
Four or more	11

Note: * N is less than 134 as all pupils did not answer every question.

Table 8.7: *Number of secondary schools visited*

Number of schools	Percentage of pupils* (N = 134)
None	19
One	32
Two	30
Three	16
Four or more	4

Note: * Percentage adds up to more than 100 because of rounding.

probably unfamiliar secondary school to which they were due to transfer is, not surprisingly, of crucial importance to the children themselves. This ties up with comments made by parents about why their children want to go to particular secondary schools.

Pupils were asked whether they had looked at any booklets about secondary schools; over two-thirds (68 per cent) reported that they had. Table 8.6 gives the number of brochures that they reported having read. Around a third of the pupils reported that they had not read any brochures; two-fifths had read one or two brochures, and over a quarter had read three or more.

Over eight out of ten pupils (82 per cent) had visited prospective secondary schools to try and find out whether it was a school they might like to attend. Nearly one-fifth of the pupils had not visited any secondary schools. About one-third had visited one (32 per cent) or two schools (30 per cent). One-fifth of the pupils had visited three or more schools.

Conclusions

In this chapter we have looked at what the pupils considered to be the key issues in relation to their thinking about and 'choosing' a school. This chapter is based upon a bigger response rate among the children than was obtained with the parents of the target children in the main sample. There are, therefore, almost twice as many children who responded than parents. However, the questions asked here were answered in written form rather than orally and may in both senses contribute to some of the differences that we have found.

As we have already noted above, around one-fifth of the pupils in the study wanted to go to an LEA mixed school and the same proportion to an LEA all girls' school. Slightly more pupils than parents preferred a grant-maintained school or CTC. In the vast majority of cases (over eight out of ten cases), the child and mother named the same school as their preferred school. This means that one in five children did *not* agree with their mother and preferred a different school to the one named. In just under two-thirds of cases, the child and father named the same school. In other words, even more children disagreed with their father and named a different school. The majority of pupils had talked to their parents 'a great deal', or 'quite a lot', about which secondary school to choose.

Over two-fifths of the pupils reported that they would prefer to go to a mixed school, but two fifths of the *girls* indicated that they would like to go to a single-sex girls' school. Very few boys reported that they would want to go to an all boys' school. A variety of reasons were offered for these various choices. In the case of girls it largely related to educational and social factors.

The main links with secondary schools were that other pupils from their primary school wanted to go there and that friends wanted to go there. About one-third of the pupils had not read any brochures, with about two-fifths having read one or two. Eight out of ten pupils had visited prospective secondary schools.

Some interesting differences between different groups of pupils emerged, with boys feeling that good computing and sports facilities were important considerations and more girls than boys thinking that good music facilities and friendly teachers were important considerations in their choice of a secondary school. Several differences between pupils in the two boroughs emerged, with more in Wandsworth feeling that a nice uniform was important and more in Camden feeling that no uniform was important. These differences are likely to be the result of the presence, or absence, of a school uniform at the child's preferred school. There were also differences between the pupils with respect to their views about bullying.

It is also interesting to note that more pupils whose parents had *not* been interviewed felt that it was important that friends should be going to their preferred secondary school. This is particularly noteworthy, as those parents who were not interviewed are less likely than those who were interviewed to be active choosers. It seems that pupils with 'non-active' parents may be more likely to go to particular schools if their friends are also going. Indeed, in the parents' study we found that more of those who were not volunteers mentioned, as an important factor in their choice of a secondary school, their child wanting to go to the school concerned. We can thus speculate that late responders are more like non-respondents than are early respondents.

Overall, our findings from the pupil questionnaire study confirm our findings from the parents' study, namely that there are some key differences in the reasons for the choice of school. In particular, girls and their parents (or rather mothers), as opposed to boys, and their parents tend to favour single-sex schools, whereas boys and their parents tend to prefer mixed schools. We have also found that the processes and procedures for decision-making take the same form, namely that mothers are almost invariably involved. The children's preferences tend to concur with their mothers' rather than their fathers' preferences.

Chapter 9

Conclusions: Choice, Control and Compromise?

Introduction

In this concluding chapter we bring together our various findings in terms of both qualitative and quantitative results, issues raised and stories presented to show how complex a social process is entailed in choosing a secondary school. We aim to set our accounts against other research findings and accounts of what we have called the 'choice process' and locate them in the broader contexts to which we have referred in previous chapters.

In the earlier chapters we have discussed the context in which our study of parental and pupil 'choice' of secondary school was carried out, namely that it was conducted in the early 1990s immediately after the implementation of the 1988 Education Reform Act in England and Wales. The government's avowed intention with this act was to improve educational standards by providing more *choice* and *diversity* of schools, although this piece of legislation did not go as far as subsequent legislation, such as the 1993 Education (Schools) Act, has done in creating a diversity of contexts for the choice of education.

We were, however, interested in exploring how parents and children felt about these issues and the various processes that were entailed in thinking about preferences for, and placement in, certain secondary schools. We now hope that we may be able to shed some light on how parents will now feel about the processes of making a choice in the even more market-oriented context of the 1990s in Britain.

We ourselves chose a very particular group of families to study, namely from two inner London boroughs, also in the aftermath of the changes wrought by the 1988 Education Reform Act and in the broader context of changing family circumstances. We have provided details of the characteristics of the families of the children in the sample and presented the complex stories and findings from the two different studies. One was an interview study of those parents of the target children who themselves chose to be interviewed and the second was a questionnaire study of all the original target children.

We are indeed conscious that our sample is not representative of the socio-economic characteristics of the families in the two London boroughs from which they were drawn. Nevertheless, we know that our sample is not dissimilar in fundamental *social* characteristics to families in London and other metropolitan or inner city areas and that it gives us some clues as to the kinds of socio-economic and familial changes taking place in late twentieth-century Britain. While we clearly cannot easily generalize from this study, we can provide some suggestions about the complex nature of the social processes involved in family decision-making, especially about education and school choice. Indeed, the fact that certain types of families chose to be involved tells us something about a taste for education, as does the obverse that others chose not to be involved in the interviews. This is in itself indicative of some of the complexities of the processes of making choices about education.

In this concluding chapter, our main findings and suggestions about these complex processes are drawn from each of the chapters and discussed in the context of past research. However, we are also aware that our study was conducted in ways that make it difficult to compare with previous research, since we were interested in highlighting precisely what other researchers had tended to ignore, namely the various participants in the decision processes and the fact that we construe it as a multi-layered social process rather than an event at one point in time. However, in this latter case, we borrow from Coldron and Boulton's (1991) imaginative way of approaching the question and considering how the processes may occur. In addition, we therefore discuss a number of other issues; in particular, whether it is reasonable to assume that all parents are indeed exercising 'choice' and feel themselves in a position to see this issue of school choice as being particularly salient to them. We also point to some methodological issues relating to our two studies that problematize the notions of 'choice' as a process and 'families' as decision-making units and we therefore make suggestions for future approaches to this kind of research.

Mother Chooses?

In summary, we have found that the processes and the procedures for parents making a choice of secondary school are indeed complex and complicated. However, we can summarize our key findings by saying, first that *mothers* are almost invariably involved in those processes and procedures whatever the kind of family and child. And given the complexity of the processes and stories that we have presented, the mothers' involvement is more than based on their intuition. On the other hand, fathers are *not* invariably involved and, when they are, it is largely to do with the social and cultural characteristics of families, but not necessarily to do with the family structure, that is the fact of being a lone parent family.

We are not aware of any past research that has looked at the processes of either educational decision-making or school choice in terms of the gendered nature of parenthood. Neither has there been any research in Britain at least, as far as we are aware, on the ways in which family structures and new family forms may affect educational choices and decisions. We do know that work, variously by Dorothy Smith and Alison Griffith (1990) in Canada and Annette Lareau (1989) and Joyce Epstein (1989) in the United States, shows how difficult it is for mothers from single-parent family settings to be involved in the regular and routine activities of schools. But this kind of research work is more to do with daily involvement in schooling than the more diffuse issues to do with the processes of choice (see also David, 1993 for an extended discussion). Raywid (1985) is one of the few authors to have given consideration to choice in education in the USA but she has confined her studies to the questions of choice within schools rather than between schools and has not given consideration to parents' involvement in the processes. Indeed, most American studies do not highlight this as they are more concerned with the characteristics of those who 'choose' for various reasons to opt out of public schooling and go to 'choice schools' (see, for example, Witte, 1993).

As we have already intimated, our interviewees were predominantly women, mainly the mothers of the target children, but occasionally their grandmother or the child's sister. We had foreseen that this was likely to be the situation given the evidence of an overwhelming number of previous educational studies and those involving child-care questions (Oakley, 1981; David *et al.*, 1993). Yet these women lived in a variety of different family circumstances — as lone mother families, as two-parent households, as stepmothers or as the partner to a 'natural' father, etc. In two-fifths of the families interviewed the children who were about to transfer to secondary school were not living in a traditional 'nuclear family'; almost a quarter of the children lived with their mother alone, as we would have expected given their other family characteristics.

We have therefore shown how, in about a quarter of these lone mother families, the fathers were involved with the process of making a choice; and, as a corollary, fathers in the two-parent families were not always as frequently involved, leaving the decision to the mother. In other words, we might surmise that in some traditional two-parent families decision-making, including educational decisions, remains sex differentiated and largely a maternal responsibility. It is also the case that many mothers are reluctant to give up or renege on this responsibility. On the other hand, mothers in lone parent families might feel obliged, where possible, to involve the fathers of their children in this 'decision', showing us that it is not taken lightly, but seen as a serious matter.

Whatever the family circumstances the mother *was* involved with the processes of decision-making about her child's education, including the process of school transfer. However, the mother was rarely the only one involved; she might have done what many of the mothers referred to as 'the leg work' rather than just using her intuition or she might have shared the work with the father and/or the child. In eight out of ten families both parents (or significant adults) were taking part in the decision about which school their child should attend; over three-quarters of these parents were thinking about the same schools.

However, in nearly half of the families the mother was felt to have had the main responsibility for deciding which school the child should attend. One-fifth of the interviewees stated that both parents had had the main responsibility and in just over 10 per cent of families both parents and the child were felt to have had the main responsibility. Indeed, we have shown clearly that the child was involved with the processes of decision-making in the majority of circumstances, although it was rare indeed for the child to have been given the sole and main responsibility.

This strikes at the heart of some of the central concerns amongst families about the nature of parental responsibilities generally over children's upbringing and in particular in relation to education. One reason for mothers invariably being involved in the processes may be to do with the ways in which they accept their maternal responsibilities for child rearing and, indeed, in many contexts are reluctant to relinquish them. They find it difficult to transfer them to other family members given their situations. On the other hand, parents differ in their views as to when children should be given or accept some measure of responsibility for their own lives and education. This is indicated by the differing ways in which children were said to be included in the responsibility for making the 'choice' and by the ways in which their views were taken into account as reasons for the choice, to which we will refer again.

In fact, as a society, we are not clear about these issues and waver over the question of when children should be entitled to some personal responsibility and over what issues. Indeed, our study took place around the time that the Children Act, 1989 was being implemented, giving children greater rights than hitherto, including that of being a signatory for certain issues in their lives. In the case of school transfer, however, our target children were given neither the opportunity nor the right to fill in or even sign the transfer form in the two boroughs in which we were involved. We found small but perhaps cautiously important differences between families in terms of the 'rights' they afforded sons and daughters. This again chimes with wider social issues about when girls, as opposed to boys, should be given responsibilities in terms of their growing sexual maturity, contrasting questions such as Gillick competence for girls over contraceptive advice and the recent furore over the age of consent for heterosexual and homosexual adolescents. Our evidence here is slight but suggestive of differences, in some families, over the maturity of sons and daughters and therefore their competence to be involved in what might be seen as serious issues of decision. In the wider social and political arena, for example, children can be held responsible in courts of law for extremely serious crimes, including murder (for example the James Bulger case, where two 10-year-olds were convicted of murder) but cannot be responsible for signing, with their parents, the transfer form at age 11 for their preferred secondary school.

We found that there were differences, too, between our families in how they went about the processes of making the decision and how long they had been considering what kinds of schools to name. This means that the question of what education is about and what schooling is for was not a simple one and depended upon a variety of circumstances and issues — what we have called a multi-layered process. We considered first some immediate issues about how long families had thought about the processes and then we broadened our consideration to issues about their own circumstances and memories, hopes and expectations in an attempt to demonstrate the increasing complexity of the process.

Almost half of the parents only started thinking seriously about secondary schools when their child was in the last year of primary schooling (Year 6 or fourth year juniors); a third started thinking about this issue when she or he was in Year 5, and over a fifth had started thinking about it prior to this. Interestingly, and perhaps inevitably again, it was mothers who began the early processes of consideration by doing what amounted to the 'leg work' and the majority of these women were in two-parent households, where they might have had both the time and the inclination to take on this responsibility. Mothers on their own tended to indicate that they were only able to start the process in the last year of primary schooling.

Mobility in the sample of parents was high with nearly three-quarters having moved since their child was born. For a minority of parents the child's schooling had been a consideration when moving. Other moves may have been to do with changes in family circumstances but we did not probe into this although we were interested in how and when consideration was first given to the child's education. This kind of mobility is an important consideration for being clear about what kinds of social processes are involved in mothers' considerations of their children's upbringing and schooling.

Constraints on Mothers' Choices of School

We found that parents (or rather mothers, given that we interviewed predominantly women) do, on the whole, feel that this issue of secondary school choice has a certain salience, although they may see it only as between limited options, rather than being able to make decisive choices. The choice can be seen as being like a choice not between apples and oranges but between kinds of apple — a crab-apple versus an orange pippin. In other words, parents have to make some kind of compromise rather than be in full control over their child's life and future, including education.

This kind of finding that school choice is seen as salient to some families chimes with other recent studies in both Britain and other countries. Glenn (1989) reviewing choice arguments across six nations other than the USA for the US government, found that some parents do use choice as a way to influence their own children's educational futures, whether or not it helps other children. He argues that changes in policy do have the effect of making parents feel empowered (p. 220) even if they also have the effect of making greater inequities between families.

Nevertheless, for some of our parents in particular circumstances, the processes and procedures of their child's earlier life may have enabled them to exert some control by the time the child reaches the final year (Year 6) of state primary school. Parents have been able to exercise some influence over their child's attitudes and approaches to education through the ways in which they have reared their children. This means that at age 11 the child feels herself or himself to be in some measure of agreement with the parents over their educational future.

We found that most parents had been thinking about more than one secondary school for their children. Nearly a quarter of the parents thought about just one secondary school for their child, and, in the event, just over half of the parents applied to one school only, while just over a quarter had applied to two schools. A fifth of the parents applied to between three and five schools. In other words, this is another way of saying that parents feel that they are not entirely constrained by their situations, despite the fact that they may feel the differences on offer are between crab-apples and orange pippins rather than more exotic kinds of fruit, such as pineapples or mangoes.

Many of the procedures used by the schools and/or LEAs militate against parents feeling that they are fully in control of the process of educational decision-making, but that they have to make the best of it, or feel fatalistically resigned to it. Around half of the parents had a good understanding of the transfer procedure. However, nearly half did not and this suggests that schools (and LEAs) had not adapted to their relatively changed situations with respect to school choice. On the other hand, it could be that the families we interviewed were not sufficiently well acquainted with the intricacies of the processes and procedures. At the level of policy execution, it could be important for schools and LEAs, now firmly in the marketplace, to consider providing more 'user friendly' information for the 'customers' about secondary transfer. They could perhaps hold meetings with parents to explain what is involved, particularly in relation to secondary schools' admissions criteria.

The secondary school preferred by the parents was in fact extremely variable, illustrating again that families differ in their preferences for education and schooling even within the kinds of constrained choices that are on offer. The preferences ranged from an LEA mixed school (county or voluntary) in a quarter of families, to an LEA girls' school in around a fifth of the families and, for a very small minority, to either a mixed or single-sex county or voluntary school outside the borough. Grant-maintained schools, the city technology college in Wandsworth and private schools were mentioned by small numbers of parents. Of course, only Wandsworth parents named the one CTC in Wandsworth at the time, but grant-maintained schools were cited by parents in both boroughs.

This variety also had implications for the kinds of information that parents thought important as a basis for giving consideration to choice of school. We asked the parents for their views of this and the most frequently mentioned sources of information about the parents' preferred school were visits to the school, friends/neighbours and school information booklets. The most frequently reported links with the parents' preferred secondary school were that their child's friends were planning to go there and that their child's friends went there.

The types of information most frequently mentioned by parents, when asked what they were looking for in secondary schools, were the academic side/subjects offered, A level results, GCSE results and the general atmosphere/feel of the school. Nearly half of the parents found the school examination results useful. However, significant numbers of parents found them confusing or difficult to understand. This has implications for schools and the way in which they present their examination results. Although there is a legal require-ment to provide examination results, the format required is not readily understood by all the parents. A written description of the results and their significance could be considered. Presented in as objective a way as possible, it may well be able to convey information that parents who are not familiar with statistical presentations can comprehend.

Nearly nine out of ten parents had visited secondary schools. Frequently mentioned sources of information about secondary schools (in addition to school brochures) were friends, parents of children at secondary school, children (including siblings) and parents of children at their preferred secondary school. This information was most frequently obtained in Year 6, but by significant minorities of parents before this time. This finding also supports the point made earlier that the process of choosing a secondary school is not limited to the final year of primary schooling and primary and secondary schools should consider this in all matters related to the transfer process.

There was a trend for more parents who were in traditional family situ-ations, than those in lone mother or other non-traditional family situations, to mention that the teachers/headteacher were an important factor in their choice of secondary school (29 per cent versus 6 and 0 per cent). In other words, parents in traditional family situations may be more reliant on established educational sources than those in less conventional situations. They may also be more inclined to be members of the traditional professional classes and more attuned to educational reasoning, as others have pointed out (Fitz, 1991; and Bernstein, 1990).

In well over three-quarters of the families, the interviewee and their child's other parent (or significant adult) agreed about the choice of the school. For various reasons, nearly a quarter of the parents felt that they had had to compromise about the secondary school(s) to which they had applied. Over eight out of ten parents indicated that their children wanted to go to the same school as their parents wanted them to attend. In over half the cases, the child was reported to like this school because friends were going there. More Camden than Wandsworth parents reported that their child liked his or her preferred school because friends were going there (67 versus 39 per cent).

Although the child's wishes were not frequently reported to be an important reason for choosing a particular school, children were often hoping to go to the same school as friends. It is possible that schools are being selected by like-minded parents for similar reasons with the 'knock on' effect that their children will go to the same schools as friends — who may well be of a similar social group.

In relation to other research studies, our findings reveal that parents report that the 'child's wishes' occurs less frequently as an important reason than in some other studies (e.g. West and Varlaam, 1991). This is discussed further below, but suffice it to say, at this stage, that the sample in the present study was not as varied, in terms of its social class make-up as in the study by West and Varlaam. The fact that Coldron and Boulton also found that the child's preference was more likely to be cited by those in manual occupations than others lends support to this notion. Ball *et al.* (1994) make a similar point — namely that for working-class parents the child's wishes are often more decisive, while for middle-class parents the child's input to the process is more limited (see also West, 1993).

Parents' Reasons for Preferring or Rejecting Schools

We have also shown that parents feel that there is some 'bottom line' about the various alternatives or options on offer whatever the constraints upon these processes and decisions. They *do* regard certain schools and certain characteristics of some schools as being unacceptable. To refer back to our apple analogy, it may be that many parents do not want crab-apples but favour orange pippins! They are able to tell us clearly what it is that they prefer about the schools they opt for and, on the other hand, what they do not like about the schools they did not opt for or rejected.

The reasons most frequently mentioned for liking the preferred school were its subjects/facilities (mentioned by over two-fifths of the parents), the school's atmosphere/ethos and academic results (each mentioned by over a quarter of parents) and first impressions (mentioned by just under a quarter). Moreover, there are three features of schools that, taken together, can be positively identified as being the reasons for opting for a particular school — what we have called the three Ps — the academic results or *performance*; the atmosphere/ethos or *pleasant feel*; and the school's location or *proximity to home*. However, we do not wish to argue that any one of these three features/factors taken on its own is the *main* reason for choice, but these three best approximate the *amalgam* of factors that parents presented as reasons or factors associated with their 'choice' for opting for particular schools. These factors have all in various ways been identified in other research studies. Elliott (1982), in an early study of school choice in England after changes in the law, cited proximity to home as a major reason for secondary school choice. He also identified academic results as being important for some parents. Coldron and Boulton looked at the processes of decision-making and revealed that a child's happiness was a major criterion of parental choice.

No significant differences between parents from different ethnic groups emerged. However, there was a trend for more white and Asian than black parents to mention that the ethos/atmosphere or *pleasant feel* of the school was an important factor in their choice of secondary school (38 and 25 per cent versus 0 per cent), and more white than black or Asian parents mentioned *proximity to home* as an important factor (32 per cent versus 11 and 0 per cent).

More parents where the father was from a non-manual rather than a skilled manual or semi-skilled/unskilled occupational background liked the school(s) they were applying to because of the environment/buildings (33 per cent versus 5 and 13 per cent); did not want their child to go to particular schools because they disliked what they saw (63 per cent versus 8 and 33 per cent); reported that their child liked his or her preferred school because of what she or he had seen (52 per cent versus 14 and 25 per cent) and indicated that the atmosphere/ethos or pleasant feel was an important factor in their choice (53 per cent versus 27 and 0 per cent).

Similarly, more parents, where the mother was in professional/managerial/technical and in other non-manual occupations than in manual occupations, reported that the atmosphere/ethos or *pleasant feel* of the school was an important factor in their choice of a school (48 and 31 per cent versus 0 per cent). More parents, where the mother was in professional/managerial/technical employment than in other non-manual or in manual employment, liked the school(s) they were applying to because of the way teaching was organized (24 per cent versus 3 and 0 per cent).

However, we found that the three Ps — performance, pleasant feel and proximity to home — are together the most frequently occurring important reasons offered by parents, closely followed by the subjects offered. The reasons most frequently mentioned as most important were the school's academic record/good education, the child's wishes/happiness and the school's location. Organizational factors were most frequently mentioned as second and third most important reasons. It should, however, be noted that a wide variety of reasons were given in idiosyncratic combinations.

A number of interesting differences between parents of girls and boys and other groups of parents are also raised. Moreover, there were clear *gender* differences in reasons; what predominates as a factor for *girls* is *single-sex schooling,* while *facilities in mixed schools* predominates as a factor for *boys.* More parents of girls than boys liked the school(s) they were applying to because they were small (24 versus 3 per cent) and because they were single sex (27 versus 3 per cent). More parents of boys than girls reported that an important factor in their choice of secondary school for their child was that they liked what they saw (22 versus 0 per cent). More parents of boys than girls reported that their child liked the facilities at her or his preferred school (40 versus 12 per cent).

The child's sex was felt to have affected the actual preferred choice of school for half of the parents. Of these, half said that they would want a single-sex school for a girl, but a mixed school for a boy. This finding supports that of West and Varlaam (1991), which was also carried out in inner London, who also found that single-sex schooling for girls was an important factor.

As we noted above, the parents on the whole could distinguish positive and negative factors about the schools on offer. Many of them gave strong reasons for not wanting certain schools — just as they might have told us why they would not want crab-apples as opposed to orange pippins! About three-quarters of the parents said that there were schools they did not want their child to attend. The most frequently mentioned reasons were poor discipline/behaviour, the school's bad reputation and that they disliked what they saw.

The reasons presented for parents *not* wanting pupils to go to certain schools were also differentiated on gender lines. More parents of boys than girls did not want their child to go to particular schools because of the discipline/behaviour of pupils there (69 versus 47 per cent). More parents, who were lone mothers or in other non-traditional family situations (lone fathers, mother and partner) than those in mother and father situations, reported that they did not want their child to go to particular schools because they disliked what they saw (64 and 67 per cent versus 25 per cent).

Issues of Discipline and Parents' Own Educational Experiences and Expectations

We also considered, in depth, the issue of 'discipline', and concluded that some concept of discipline — or more explicitly, the wider matter of social order and control — concerns almost all parents. It is not only a negative factor; many parents see the notion of children learning about the limits of behaviour as extremely important, although they have different areas of concern and see different purposes for discipline. In other words, many parents are concerned about instilling some notion of self-discipline and/or deference to authority into their children, either at home or at school and through explicit or implicit forms of upbringing. This links clearly with Ribbens' other study of mothers' attitudes to child rearing in general (1994, forthcoming). We also show that what parents mean by 'discipline' is highly variable and is often linked with their values and broader perspectives on life, such as religious views.

However, the parents in our study link their views of 'discipline' with their own experiences of school and upbringing. This was part of our attempt to demonstrate the complexity of the social process and indeed to broaden the picture of the way in which school choice is a multi-layered process. We also explored in some detail the ways in which memories of their own schooldays influenced parents' thoughts about their children's education. For the majority of parents, their own school experiences were indeed considered relevant to how they thought about their children's education. Memories of schooldays evoked strong feelings in many people. We were rather saddened to find that almost one-fifth of those who answered this question said there was nothing at all from their own schooldays that they would want to be repeated for their children. By contrast, 18 per cent had had such good experiences of school that there was nothing they would want to be different for their children.

It was quite clear, then, that different experiences of education, and disciplinary approaches in particular, influenced how parents thought about schools for their children. Again, their approaches were highly variable. Relationships with teachers and issues of discipline were the two areas that were most frequently discussed and some strong attitudes emerged against corporal punishment. Other issues raised by several parents were mixed versus single-sex schooling, relationships with peers and general attitudes of encouragement of children. More narrowly educational issues received much less attention in the course of these discussions of old memories of their schooling.

We also examined parents' hopes and expectations for their child's education beyond secondary schooling. What was particularly striking here was the extent to which all parents wanted their children to continue into further and higher education. In other words, all parents in this sample viewed education as a 'good thing'. However, this may have something to do with the particular characteristics of our sample, tending towards the middle classes and skilled working class.

More generally, we also considered the parents' general views about different types of education, both generally in terms of such issues as comprehensive schooling, independent schooling and in terms of the borough's own education policies. Curiously, given the points made above about our sample, many of the parents were relatively unclear about the particular characteristics of schools and party politics on education. We surmise that this apparent indifference has to do with the fact that the majority of our sample are women who are more interested in issues of everyday life than in global party politics, as has been found by other researchers (Lovenduvski *et al.*, 1993).

What was most interesting to us was the fact that parents' different experiences in their own education, and in their present situations and political orientations, had such diverse effects upon school choices and general views of schooling. In other words, although our sample of families tended to be rather 'mainstream' and to exclude the semi-skilled, unskilled and other disaffected and marginal groups, nevertheless there was an enormous variety and diversity of approaches to these issues of educational decision-making. This partly leads us to the conclusion that the issues themselves are so intricately interwoven with people's other social issues and their lives in general that there is no easy summary of how the process of school choice can be approached.

The Pupils' Stories of Choice

We have also looked separately at the ways in which children approached the question of school choice. It is important, however, to note that the children whom we questioned composed our original target group and that for about half of the ones who answered our questionnaire, their parents also contributed to the study, and are the ones on whom we have based the majority of our analysis. What we found is that there is indeed considerable consistency between the study of the parents and the study of the children. Similar themes and issues emerged from both studies, in particular in terms of reasons for choice of preferred school and the ways in which children were involved in the processes of decision-making.

First, it is significant that there were differences between the two groups of pupils questioned — those whose parents participated in the research and those whose parents had not — in terms of their overall approaches to the reasons for choosing schools. This adds to our feeling that our parent sample was concerned with issues to do with education, and that they were keen to give serious consideration to factors about it, despite the fact that we have just pointed to the enormous diversity in the ways in which they went about it. More pupils of the interviewed parents gave educational reasons for their preferred school. More pupils whose parents had not been interviewed felt that it was important that friends should be going to their preferred secondary school. This particular finding has important methodological implications that are discussed below.

Second, the majority of pupils talked to their parents about secondary schools 'a great deal' or 'quite a lot'. In over eight out of ten children, the child and mother named the same school as their preferred school; in just under two-thirds of cases, the child and father named the same school. This finding is of particular interest in the context of who has the 'main responsibility' for choosing a secondary school and again points to the crucial role played by the mother. In other words, the child appears, from this pupil study, to be more in touch with the mother's wishes than the father's. This also adds to our view of the ways in which maternal responsibility is assumed. It also shows, however, that almost one-fifth of pupils did not agree with the 'choice' that had been made on their behalf.

The most frequently mentioned factors that pupils endorsed as important reasons for wanting to go to a particular secondary school were a good education, good art facilities and friendly teachers. Good science facilities, good computing facilities, good sports facilities and no bullying were all endorsed by over eight out of ten pupils. Similar findings were also obtained by West *et al.* (1991) in an outer London LEA. Factors that pupils felt would put them off particular schools included bullying and a threatening atmosphere.

We found that around one-fifth of the pupils in the study wanted to go to an LEA mixed or all girls' school. Slightly more pupils than parents preferred a grant-maintained school or CTC. Over two-fifths of the pupils reported that they would prefer to go to a mixed school, and over one-fifth indicated that they would like to go to a single-sex girls' school; very few boys reported that they would want to go to an all boys' school.

The main links with secondary schools were that other pupils from their primary school wanted to go there and that friends wanted to go there. About one-third of the pupils had not read any brochures, with about two-fifths having read one or two. Eight out of ten pupils had visited prospective secondary schools.

Some interesting differences between different groups of pupils emerged, with boys feeling that good computing and sports facilities were important considerations and more girls than boys thinking that good music facilities and friendly teachers were important considerations in their choice of a secondary school.

Several differences between pupils in the two boroughs emerged, with more in Wandsworth feeling that a nice uniform was important and more in Camden feeling that no uniform is important. These differences are likely to be the result of the presence or absence of a school uniform at the child's preferred school. Thus the kinds of differences that emerged between the pupils were similar to those cited by the parents, with a particular set of gender differences appearing to be key. Boys tended to prefer certain facilities and mixed schools, as did the parents of boys, while girls tended to consider ethos and atmosphere and also single-sex schools, as did their parents. Children's wishes had clearly played a part for the children as the parents had also reported. Despite the fact that we have seen the whole process as complex there are some relatively constant and clear themes that are revealed in both the parents' and pupils' stories.

Methodological Issues

A number of interesting differences emerged in our studies of parental and pupil choice of secondary schools that have methodological implications. As mentioned above, our sample of parents was not statistically representative of the boroughs in which the studies took place in terms of its social and ethnic/racial composition; this is largely accounted for by the fact that the response rate for the interviews with parents was only around a half. However, we have argued that, given the complexity of the issues and social processes involved, we can find clear clues to the themes and issues for parents in late twentieth-century Britain. We return to this issue again below.

Of the parents who were interviewed there were differences between those who volunteered to be interviewed (that is those who responded to the letters sent out) and those who were interviewed subsequently. Two important (and statistically significant) results emerged, namely that more parents who volunteered — over a quarter compared with 3 per cent — reported that the teachers or headteacher at the school was an important factor in their choice of school. In addition, more parents — about a fifth compared with none — who did *not* volunteer mentioned as an important factor their child wanting to go to the school concerned.

This links with our finding from the pupil study that more pupils whose parents were not interviewed wanted to go to schools because their friends went there. In other words, children's wishes and those of their friends were more important to those who were relatively reluctant to be involved in the study than where parents were enthusiastic and keen to consider a range of educational issues.

Moreover there were some differences between the parents who were early volunteers to be interviewed and those who had to be pressed. One of the interviewers reported that her first four early volunteers had all had bad experiences of schooling themselves, and were all 'active choosers' now in relation to their children's schooling. She provided this vignette to illustrate the point:

> Mrs M lived in a large, well-furnished, older terraced house. She had had bad experiences of school herself, in private education. She presented her daughter as being a bright student, and was very active about the process of choosing her secondary school. She described the local state system as only providing one possibility and that was at some distance. Consequently they were applying for private schools or schools in other boroughs: 'We went and viewed every school in the area and she is actually sitting [exams] for all those'.

These differences indicate that parents with sons or daughters, those from different social backgrounds and indeed those who have different attitudes to involvement in research studies of this type have different views on the reasons for choosing particular schools; the findings indicate that issues such as these need to be addressed in any study examining the choice process. It is not always possible to pinpoint accurately how and why differences exist, but given the differences observed, they cannot be ignored and further qualitative research may be able to shed light on issues such as these.

The results from the survey of pupils also lend support to the notion that the parents who were interviewed were more 'active choosers' than those who did not participate. As noted above, almost all the pupils in the five schools completed a questionnaire, and we found that more pupils whose parents had not been interviewed than those whose parents had been interviewed re-ported that friends going to a particular secondary school would make them want to go to that school.

It would appear that pupils with parents who are not active choosers may be more likely to go to particular schools if their friends are going. This seems to support other research findings on the differences between middle-class and working-class families in terms of the factors that they look for in choosing schools. Middle-class families appear to show more interest in strictly educational factors, including ethos or atmosphere and buildings, whereas working-class families appear to be more concerned with reasons to do with their children's 'happiness' or perhaps in terms of the social experience of schooling and the significance of neighbourhood and social networks as ways of getting by in life.

However, we should also note that our study has rendered problematic issues to do with traditional definitions of social class. Although we have mentioned that our study is 'more middle class' than we might have expected and that we have missed out the unskilled and semi-skilled working classes so that it is not statistically representative of the characteristics of the two LEAs, there is also a thorny issue of whether or not current definitions of class accord with traditional notions. In other words, the kinds of economic and social changes going on have made the characteristics of many forms of employment difficult to identify. Indeed, women's occupations are usually defined in ways that make them appear more middle class in that they are said to be non-manual. However, they may well not have the traditional characteristics of non-manual service occupations. We have also shown how many of our mothers have partners who have more traditionally defined skilled working-class occupations. So we need to pay careful attention to the changing definitions and facts of the class structure in order to interpret our findings fully.

These findings have implications for research in investigating parental choice of school. Our parent study, although achieving an acceptable response rate in comparison with other similar research (Edwards *et al.*, 1989), was not as representative in terms of its social and ethnic characteristics as we had hoped, and indeed some of the findings in relation to factors important in the choice process do not replicate those found elsewhere by one of the authors (West and Varlaam, 1991), in particular the finding in the earlier study that the child wanting to go to the school is the most frequently reported important reason to emerge; in this earlier study a sample of parents representative of the year group of the primary schools in the sample was targeted and as a result, the overall sample of parents was more statistically representative of the parents in inner London in terms of their social and ethnic characteristics.

In order to establish whether the findings from our current study represent a change in factors considered to be important when choosing secondary schools, perhaps as a result of the increased focus by the government and the media on examination results, or whether they are as a result of the charac-teristics of the sample, further research using a more representative sample of parents is needed. The targeting of particular groups of parents, to ensure that 'active' and 'less active' parents are included in studies of parental choice is worthy of serious consideration, difficult though that would appear to be.

The pupils themselves are also a valuable source of information about the process of choosing secondary schools. Our research shows that children in Year 6 are able to provide at times quite complex information. Moreover, the response rate is likely to be high and to be representative. There are, however, draw-backs to using questionnaires with pupils, one of which is that their responses may need further probing to enable 'richer' qualitative data to be obtained. The other is that it is not as easy to ask questions relating to pupils' backgrounds (however other research studies have done this although with slightly older pupils; see West *et al.*, 1991). Of course, different factors might be prioritized if pupils were to discuss their reasons spontaneously and without prompting.

Choosing or Chosen; Control or Compromise?

This study of choice of secondary schools from both the parents' and children's perspectives has shown how the choice process is largely the responsibility of the mother; it has also shown that the concept of responsibility is one that needs to be further elaborated — perhaps into more specifically defined subconcepts such as 'sole' responsibility or 'main' or 'final' responsibility. Moreover, we believe that the concepts of responsibility for child rearing as well as education need more careful elucidation and mapping of the boundaries between the public and private, the formal and informal, men and women and in different family contexts.

We set out to illustrate that the concept of the 'family' is problematic in the current context of both family and socio-economic changes. We hope to have clearly illustrated this even from such a small-scale study. We have revealed that family diversity replicates and is replicated in social and educational diversity. No single lone mother family is exactly the same as another and neither is there clear continuity between traditional two-parent families.

These differences are not only because families are complex and are currently in complicated and changing times. It is also because the issue we chose to study is also complex; the choice process itself is a multi-faceted one, taking place for most families over a year or more and generally involving the use of a wide variety of information sources as well as a plethora of experiences over a much greater time span. At times, and for some parents, the 'choice' process appears to involve an active and careful search for relevant information, which is then examined and evaluated, leading to a rational and clearcut decision. At other times, and for other parents, the term 'choice' appears to be less relevant. Instead, we see parents and children as participating in extensive networks of social relations that provide some relevant information and shape perceptions of schools. In addition, and importantly, the experience of school as a social and emotional matter, as well as a strictly educational matter, is clearly an important consideration. Continuity of social relations and neighbourhood links may thus be valued alongside the more explicit educational goals that parents also value.

Examination results are a significant issue for 'choice' as a rational matter. Although considered an important and, in the political arena at the moment, a critical source of information, they are not always readily understood and it would seem desirable for them to be explained to parents in non-technical language and provided with 'health warnings' so that parents are aware that they may well not be comparing like with like (see West, 1992b). If exam results are to become an essential element in the formal and official processes of 'school choice' then the ways in which they are presented needs far more careful consideration (see also West *et al.*, 1995 forthcoming).

However, we cannot assert from this study that parents do regard examination results as the critical or vital element in the process or even as essential in the marketplace. There is no one piece of information that we have found to be outstandingly important for all parents as a basis for decision-making.

The most frequently reported important factors that parents consider when making a decision as to which secondary school a child should attend are what we have called the three Ps — namely the school's performance in terms of academic results, the pleasant feel of the school and the proximity of the school. As suggested elsewhere (West, 1994), some of these factors may be of overriding importance and may be either 'structural' or 'dynamic' — 'structural' characteristics, such as the type of school (for example, mixed or single-sex) or its location, being less amenable to change than more 'dynamic' factors such as the school's examination results.

Some issues are of more relevance to particular groups of parents than others — in particular, single-sex schools for girls and school facilities for boys. The issue of discipline is one that is important to almost all parents, but one that, our analysis shows, is not one that necessarily has negative connotations; it is of concern to almost all parents, but conceptions of what it constitutes vary widely. It is far more important as an issue with respect to parents' different and highly variable conceptions of what constitutes 'good upbringing' as well as 'good education': how to create effective and moral adults for the next generation.

Almost all the pupils themselves report that a 'good education' would make them want to go to a particular school. In relation to other factors, there were some interesting differences between girls and boys, with girls being more concerned that the teachers should be friendly and more boys being concerned about computing and sports facilities. Overall, however, by the time they are nearly adolescents children have been imbued with a particular sense of what is right and proper with respect to schools. It is clear that education has a high priority among not only parents but also children. This leads us to the conclusion that it would be important to pursue a study of children's views of the processes of educational choice rather than replicate our more limited study of choice here as a period of decision-making.

Overall, our two studies have provided considerable insight into the processes involved in choosing secondary schools and issues that parents and their children take into account. It is evident that families do not take these issues lightly but invest considerable amounts of time and energy into thinking about education and particular schools. However, we have found it hard to disentangle the ways in which families go about this from the broader ways in which families live their lives and give consideration to living in constrained circumstances. Inevitably for some families thinking about particular schools is a luxury that they are unable to afford. For others it is so important that it cannot be left to the vagaries of circumstance or constraints of time and money. The difference between families, in those who find it hard to give it consideration and those who would not abrogate the responsibility, has more to do with the ways in which they are now positioned with respect to the educational market place than with their own wishes and desires. Diversity and choice in education has indeed created and exacerbated social and family diversity.

References

ADLER, M., PETCH, A. and TWEEDIE, J. (1989) *Parental Choice and Educational Policy*, Edinburgh, Edinburgh University Press.

ARBER, S., DALE, A. and GILBERT, G.N. (1986) 'The limitations of existing social classifications for women', in JACOBY, A. (Ed.) *The Measurement of Social Class*, London, Social Research Association.

BAKER, K. (1994) *Choice and Motherhood: Who's in Control?* Unpublished Dissertation, School of Health Care Studies, Oxford Brookes University.

BALL, S. and BOWE, R. (1991) 'Micropolitics of radical change: Budgets, management and control in British Schools', in BLASE, J. (Ed.) *The Politics of School Life*, London, Sage.

BALL, S. (1993) 'Education markets, choice and social class: The market as a class strategy in the UK and USA', *British Journal of the Sociology of Education*, **14**, 1, pp. 3–21.

BALL, S.J., BOWE, R. and GEWIRTZ, S. (1994) 'Circuits of schooling: A sociological exploration of parental choice in social class contexts', *Sociological Review*, (forthcoming).

BELL, R. and MACBETH, A. (1989) 'Parent–School Relationships', in *Exploring Educational Issues*, Milton Keynes, Open University.

BELL, L. and RIBBENS, J. (1994) 'Isolated housewives and complex maternal worlds? The significance of social contacts between women with young children in industrial societies', *Sociological Review*, **42**, 2, pp. 227–62.

BELLAH, R.N., MADSEN, R., SULLIVAN, W.M., SWIDLER, A. and TIPON, S. (1985) *Habits of the Heart: Individualism and Commitment in American Family Life*, Berkeley, University of California Press.

BERGER, P. and BERGER, B. (1984) *The War over the Family: Capturing the Middle Ground*, Harmondsworth, Penguin.

BERNSTEIN, B. (1990) *The Structuring of Pedagogic Discourse*, London, Routledge and Kegan Paul.

BERTAUX, D. (1991) 'From methodological monopoly to pluralism in the sociology of social mobility', in DEX, S. (Ed.) *Life and Work History Analyses: Qualitative and Quantitative Developments*, London, Routledge.

BJORNBERG, U. (Ed.) (1992) *European Parents in the 1990s: Contradictions and Comparisons*, New Brunswick, Transaction Publishers.

Bowe, R. and Ball, S. with Gold, A. (1993) *Reforming Education and Changing Schools*, London, Routledge.

Bowe, R., Gewirtz, S. and Ball, S. (1994) 'Captured by the discourse? Issues and concerns in researching parental choice', *British Journal of the Sociology of Education*, **15**, 1, pp. 63–79.

Brannen, J. and Moss, P. (1991) *Managing Mothers: Dual Earner Households after Maternity Leave*, London, Unwin Hyman.

Brannen, J. (Ed.) (1992) *Mixing Methods: Qualitative and Quantitative Research*, London, Gower.

Brown, L.M. and Gilligan, C. (1992) *Meeting at the Crossroads: Women's Psychology and Girls' Development*, Cambridge, MA, Harvard University Press.

Bryman, A. (1988) *Quantity and Quality in Social Research*, London, Unwin Hyman.

Central Statistical Office (1992) *Social Trends*, No. 22, London, HMSO.

Cohen, B. (1988) *Caring for Children: Services and Policies for Childcare and Equal Opportunities in the UK*, London, Commission of the European Communities.

Cohen, B. and Fraser, N. (1993) *Childcare in a Modern Welfare System. Towards a New National Policy*, London, Institute of Public Policy Research.

Coldron, J. and Boulton, P. (1991) 'Happiness as a criterion of parents' choice of school', *Journal of Education Policy*, **6**, 2, pp. 169–78.

Crittenden, B. (1988) *Parents, the State and the Right to Educate*, Carlton, Victoria, Melbourne University Press.

Dale, A., Gilbert, G.N. and Arber, S. (1983) *Alternative Approaches to the Measurement of Social Class for Women and Families*, Report to the Equal Opportunities Commission, October 1983.

Darling-Hammond, L. and Kirby, S. with Schlegel, P. (1985) *Tuition Tax Deductions and Parent School Choice: A Case Study of Minnesota*, Santa Monica, Rand Corporation.

David, M. (1978) 'The family-education couple: Towards an analysis of the William Tyndale dispute', in Littlejohn, G., Smart, B., Wakeford, J. and Yuval-Davis, N. (Eds) *Power and the State*, London, Croom Helm.

David, M. (1986) 'Moral and maternal: The family in the right', in Levitas, R. (Ed.) *The Ideology of the New Right*, Cambridge, Polity Press.

David, M.E. (1993a) *Parents, Gender and Education Reform,* Oxford, Polity Press.

David, M.E. (1993b) 'The citizen's voice in education', in Page, R. and Baldock, J. (Eds) *Social Policy Review 5*, University of Kent, Social Policy Association.

David, M.E., Edwards, R., Hughes, M. and Ribbens, J. (1993) *Mothers & Education Inside Out? Exploring Family-Education Policy and Experience*, London, Macmillan.

Davies, J. (Ed.) (1993) *The Family: Is it Just Another Lifestyle Choice?*, London, IEA Health and Welfare Unit, Choice in Welfare No. 15.

Department for Education (1992) *Choice and Diversity: A New Framework for Schools*, Cm 2021, London, HMSO.

Department of Education and Science (1991) *You and Your Child's Education*, London, HMSO.

Douglas, J.W.B. *et al.* (1967) *The Home and the School: A Study of Ability and Attainment in the Primary School*, London, Panther, first published 1964.

Echols, F., McPherson, A. and Willms, D. (1990) 'Parental choice in Scotland', *Journal of Educational Policy*, **5**, 3, pp. 207–22.

Edwards, R. (1990) 'Connecting method and epistemology: A white woman interviewing Black women', *Women's Studies International Forum*, **13**, 5, pp. 447–90.

Edwards, R. (1993) *Mature Women Students: Separating or Connecting Family and Education*, London, Taylor and Francis.

Edwards, T., Fitz, J. and Whitty, G. (1989) *The State and Private Education: An Evaluation of the Assisted Places Scheme*, Basingstoke, Falmer Press.

Elliott, J. (1981) 'How do parents choose and judge secondary schools?', in Cambridge Accountability Project, *A School in the Market Place*, Cambridge, University of Cambridge Institute of Education.

Elliott, J., Bridges, D., Gibson, R. and Nias, J. (1981) *School Accountability*, London, Grant McIntyre.

Elliott, J. (1982) 'How do parents choose and judge secondary schools?', in McCormack, R. (Ed.) (1982) *Calling Education to Account*, London, Heinemann Educational.

Epstein, J. (1990) 'School and family connections: Theory, research and implications for integrating sociologies of education and family', *Marriage and Family Review*, **15**, 1–2, pp. 99–126.

Fitz, J. (1991) 'From policy to workable scheme: Grant-maintained schools and the DES', *International Studies in the Sociology of Education*, **1**, pp. 129–53.

Fox, I. (1985) *Private Schools and Public Issues: The parents' view*, Basingstoke, Macmillan Press.

Giddens, A. (1992) *The Transformation of Intimacy. Sexuality, Love and Eroticism in Modern Societies*, Cambridge, Polity Press.

Ginsburg, N. (1992) *Divisions of Welfare*, London, Sage.

Glatter, R. and Woods, P. (1993) 'Competitive Arenas in Education. Studying the impact of enhanced competition and choice on parents and schools', paper presented at a conference on Quasi markets in public service delivery, SAUS, University of Bristol, 22–24 March.

Glenn, C. (1989) *Choice of Schools in 6 Nations*, Washington, DC, US Department of Education.

Goldthorpe, J.H. (1982) 'On the service class, its formation and future', in Giddens, A. and MacKenzie, G. (Eds) *Social Class and the Division of Labour*, Cambridge, Cambridge University Press.

Goldthorpe, J.H. (1983) 'Women and class analysis: In defence of the conventional view', *Sociology*, **18**, 2, pp. 159–70.

Griffith, A. and Smith, D. (1990) '"What did you do in school today?" Mothering,

Schooling, and Social Class', in *Perspectives on Social Problems*, **2**, pp. 3–24, JAI Press Inc.

GUTHRIE, J.W. and PIERCE, L.C. (1990) 'The international economy and national education reform: A comparison of education reforms in the US and GB', *Oxford Review of Education*, **16**, pp. 179–204.

HALPIN, D., POWER, S. and FITZ, J. (1991) 'Grant-maintained schools: making a difference without being different', *British Journal of Educational Studies*, **39**, 4, pp. 409–24.

HALSEY, A.H. (1992) Foreword in DENNIS, N. and ERDOS, G. *Families without Fatherhood*, London, IEA Health and Welfare Unit, Choice in Welfare No. 12.

HARGREAVES, D. (1994) *Improving London's Secondary Schools*, Report, London, ILEA.

HEATH, A. and BRITTEN, N. (1984) 'Women's jobs do make a difference', *Sociology*, **18**, 4, pp. 475–90.

HIRSCHMAN, A.O. (1989) 'Exit, voice and loyalty: further reflections and a survey of recent contributions', in HIRSCHMAN, A.O. (Ed.) *Essays in Trespassing*, Cambridge, Cambridge University Press, pp. 236–45.

HUGHES, M., WIKELEY, F. and NASH, T. (1990) *Parents and the National Curriculum: An Interim Report*, School of Education, University of Exeter.

HUNTER, J. (1991) 'Parental Choice of Secondary School', *Educational Research*, **33**, 1, pp. 31–41.

INNER LONDON EDUCATION AUTHORITY (1989) *1989 Educational Priority Indices*, RS 1254/89, London, ILEA.

JACKSON, B. and COOPER, B. (1989) 'Parent choice and empowerment: New roles for parents', *Urban Education*, **24**, 3, pp. 263–86.

JOSHI, H. (1991) 'Sex and motherhood as handicaps in the labour market', in MACLEAN, M. and GROVES, D. (Eds) *Women's Issues in Social Policy*, London, Routledge.

KAHAN, M., BUTLER, D. and STOKES, D. (1966) 'On the analytical division of social class', *British Journal of Sociology*, **17**, pp. 122–32.

KELLY, G. (1992) 'Debates and trends in comparative education', in ARNOVE, R. *et al. Emergent Issues in Education: Comparative Perspectives*, Albany, State University of New York Press.

KENWAY, J., BIGUM, C. and FITZCLARENCE, L. (1993) 'Marketing education in the postmodern age', *Journal of Education Policy*, **8**, pp. 105–23.

LAWTON, D. *et al.* (1987) *Choice and Control in Education*, London, Heinemann.

LAREAU, A. (1989) *Home Advantage: Social Class and Parental Intervention in Elementary Education*, London, Falmer Press.

LE GRAND, J. (1991) 'Quasi-markets and social policy', *Economic Journal 101*, pp. 1256–67.

LE GRAND, J. and BARTLETT, W. (1993) *Quasi-Markets and Social Policy*, London, Macmillan.

LOVENDUVSKI, J. and RANDALL, V. (1993) *Contemporary Feminist Politics*, Oxford, Oxford University Press.

MACBETH, A. (1984) *The Child Between: A Report on School–Family Relations in the Countries of the European Community*, Luxembourg, Office for Official Publications of the European Communities.

MACBETH, A., STRACHAN, D. and MACAULAY, C. (1986) *Parental Choice of School*, Glasgow Department of Education, University of Glasgow.

MARSH, C. (1986) 'Occupationally-based measures of social class', in JACOBY, A. (Ed.) *The Measurement of Social Class*, Social Research Association, London.

MARSHALL, G., NEWBY, H., ROSE, D. and VOGEL, C. (1988) *Social Class in Modern Britain*, London, Hutchinson.

McCORMACK, R., BYNNER, J., CLIFT, P., JAMES, M. and BROWN, C.M. (Eds) (1982). *Calling Education to Account*, London, Heinemann.

MIRZA, H. (1992) *Young, Female and Black*, London, Routledge.

MORRIS, R. (1993) *Choice of School: A survey 1992–3*, London, Association of Metropolitan Authorities.

MORTIMORE, P., SAMMONS, P., STOLL, L., LEWIS, D. and ECOB, R. (1988) *School Matters: The junior years*, Wells, Open Books.

MOSS, P. (1990) *Childcare in the European Community 1985–1990*, Women of Europe Supplements 31, Brussels, Commission of the European Communities.

NAULT, R. and UCHITELLE, S. (1982) 'School choice in the public sector: A case study of parental decision making', in MANLEY-CASIMIR, M. (Ed.) *Family Choice in Schooling*.

NEW, C. and DAVID, M.E. (1985) *For the Children's Sake. Making Childcare More than Women's Business*, Harmondsworth, Penguin.

NEWSON, J. and NEWSON, E. (1965) *Patterns of Infant Care in an Urban Community*, Harmondsworth, Penguin (first published by George Allen and Unwin, 1963).

OAKLEY, A. (1992) *Social Constructions of Motherhood*, London, Martin Robertson.

OSBORNE, A.F. and MORRIS, T.C. (1979) 'The rationale for a composite index of Social Class and its evaluation', *British Journal of Sociology*, **30**, pp. 39–60.

PAGE, R. and BALDOCK, J. (Eds) (1993) *Social Policy Review 5*, University of Kent, Social Policy Association.

RANSON, S. (1990) *The Politics of Reorganising Schools*, London, Unwin Hyman.

RAYWID, M.A. (1985) 'Family choice arrangements in public schools: A review of the literature', *Review of Educational Research*, **55**, pp. 435–67.

REINHARZ, S. with DAVIDMAN, L. (1992) *Feminist Methods in Social Research*, New York, Oxford University Press.

RIBBENS, J. (1989) 'Interviewing: An "unnatural situation"?' *Women's Studies International Forum*, **12**, 6, pp. 570–92.

RIBBENS, J. (1990) 'Accounting for our children: Differing perspectives on "family life" in middle income households', unpublished PhD thesis, CNAA/South Bank Polytechnic.

RIBBENS, J. (1994) (forthcoming) *Mothers and Their Children: A Feminist Sociology of Childrearing*, London, Sage.

RIST, R.C. (1980) 'Blitzkrieg ethnography: on the transformation of a method into a movement', *Educational Researcher*, **8**, 2, pp. 8–10.

ROSE, N. (1989) *Governing the Soul: The Shaping of the Private Self*, London, Routledge.

SALLIS, J. (1982) 'Beyond the market place: A parent's view', *Educational Researcher*, **8**, 2, pp. 8–10.

SMITH, D.E. and GRIFFITH, A.I. (1990) 'Coordinating the uncoordinated: Mothering, schooling, and the family wage', in *Perspectives on Social Problems*, 2, pp. 25–43, JAI Press Inc.

SOLOMOS, J. (1993) 'The local politics of racial equality policy innovation and limits to reform', in CROSS, M. and KEITH, M. (Eds) *Racism, the City and the State*, London, Routledge.

SPEY, H. (1991) 'Silenced in class: Laurie's lesson in terror', *Observer* 8 September, p. 49.

STANWORTH, M. (1984) 'Women and class analysis: A reply to John Goldthorpe', *Sociology*, **18**, 2, pp. 159–70.

STILLMAN, A. and MAYCHELL, K. (1986) *Choosing Schools: Parents, LEA's and the 1980 Education Act*, Windsor, NFER-Nelson.

STRICKLAND, S. (1991) 'Community divided by fear and anger', *The Independent*, 24 June, p. 5.

TAYLOR-GOOBY, P. (1994) 'Postmodernism and social policy: A great leap backwards?', *Journal of Social Policy*, **23**, 3, p. 20.

THOMAS, A. and DENNISON, B. (1991) 'Parental or pupil choice — who really decides in urban schools?' *Educational Management and Administration*, **19**, 4, pp. 243–49.

TRITTER, J. (1994) 'The citizen's charter: Opportunities for Users' Perspectives', *The Political Quarterly*, July.

TWEEDIE, J. (1986) 'Parental choice of school: Legislating the balance' in STILLMAN, A. (Ed.) *The Balancing Act of 1980: Parents, Politics and Education*, Slough, NFER.

TWEEDIE, J. (1989) 'The dilemmas of clients' rights in social programmes' *Law and Society Review*, **23**, 2, pp. 175–208.

UNIVERSITY OF GLASGOW (1985) *Parental Choice of School in Scotland*, Glasgow, Parental Choice Project, Department of Education, University of Glasgow.

VINCENT, C. (1992) 'Tolerating intolerance? Parental choice and race relations — the Cleveland case', *Journal of Education Policy*, **7**, 5, pp. 429–45.

WALFORD, G. (1990) *Privatization and Privilege in Education*, London, Routledge.

WALFORD, G. (1991) 'Choice of school at the first City Technology College', *Educational Studies*, **17**, 1, pp. 65–75.

WEST, A., VARLAAM, A. and MORTIMORE, P. (1984) 'Attitudes to school: A study of the parents of first year pupils', in HARGREAVES, D. (Ed.) *Improving Secondary Schools, Research Studies*, London, ILEA.

WEST, A. and VARLAAM, A. (1991) 'Choice of secondary school: Parents of junior school children', *Educational Research*, **33**, 1, pp. 22–30.

WEST, A., VARLAAM, A. and SCOTT, G. (1991) 'Choice of high schools: Pupils' perceptions', *Educational Research*, **33**, 3, pp. 205–15.

WEST, A. (1992a) *Choosing Schools: Why Do Parents Opt for Private Schools or Schools in Other LEAs?* LSE, Clare Market Papers No. 1.

WEST, A. (1992b) 'Factors affecting choice of school for middle class parents: Implications for marketing', *Educational Management and Administration*, **20**, 4, pp. 212–21.

WEST, A. and NUTTALL, D. (1992) *Choice at 11: Secondary Schools' Admissions Policies in Inner London*, LSE, Clare Market Papers, No. 2.

WEST, A. (1993) 'Choosing schools: Are different factors important for different parents?' in SMITH, M. and BUSHER, H. (Eds) *Managing Schools in an Uncertain Environment: Resources, Marketing and Power*, Sheffield, Hallam University for BEMAS.

WEST, A., DAVID, M., HAILES, J., RIBBENS, J. and HIND, A. (1993) *Choosing a Secondary School: The Parents' and Pupils' Stories*, Clare Market Paper 7, Centre for Educational Research, London School of Economics and Political Science.

WEST, A. (1994) 'Choosing schools — the consumer's perspectives', in HALSTEAD, M.J. (Ed.) *Parental Choice and Education: Principles, Policy and Practice*, London, Kogan Page.

WEST, A., DAVID, M., HAILES, J. and RIBBENS, J. (1995) (forthcoming) 'Parents and the process of choosing secondary schools: Implications for schools', *Educational Management and Administration*.

WHITTY, G. (1990) 'Market forces versus central control', in FLUDE, M. and HAMMER, M. (Eds) *The Education Reform Act 1988: Its Origins and Implications*, London, Falmer Press.

WHITTY, G., EDWARDS, T. and GEWIRTZ, S. (1993) *Specialisation and Choice in Urban Education: The City Technology College Experiment*, London, Routlege.

WICKS, M. (1991) *Social Politics 1979–1992 Family, Work and Welfare* paper to Social Policy association Annual Conference University of Nottingham, July.

WITTE, J. (1993) *The Milwaukee Parent Choice Program: The First 30 Months*, Paper given at AERA, Atlanta, Georgia 15–18 April.

Index